GOUGHY
A TOUGH LOCK TO CRACK

In memory of Uncle 'Mad Dog' Mike Gough, the Iron Man.
Robert Redford in looks and Lionel Richie in voice,
he sadly couldn't hang on long enough to see me
vindicated in court or see this book come out.

GOUGHY

A TOUGH LOCK TO CRACK

IAN GOUGH

With Peter Owen

First impression: 2015

The publishers wish to acknowledge the support of
Cyngor Llyfrau Cymru

Cover photograph: Steve Pope / Sporting Wales
Cover design: Y Lolfa

ISBN: 978 1 78461 144 6

Published and printed in Wales
on paper from well-maintained forests by
Y Lolfa Cyf., Talybont, Ceredigion SY24 5HE
website www.ylolfa.com
e-mail ylolfa@ylolfa.com
tel 01970 832 304
fax 832 782

Contents

Contents

CHAPTER 1

Highs and lows

THANKS TO MY 12 years as an international rugby player I've done plenty of interviews or Q&As for sponsors. Often this is how it goes:

Q: What has been the high point of your career?

A: Making my first appearance for Wales.

Q: And what was the low point?

A: Making my first appearance for Wales.

I remember it as if it was yesterday. Who wouldn't? Pretoria, 27 June 1998. South Africa 96 Wales 13.

I was one of six debutants that day. It was a young, inexperienced team and we were hopelessly outclassed. A Welsh record defeat. In fact the biggest defeat ever suffered by one of the eight major rugby-playing nations.

The song that they played over the PA when they scored a try was 'Tubthumping', by Chumbawumba. I knew that song off by heart by the end of the game.

I think it was Garin Jenkins who said to me as I was boarding the plane home, "Well done, Ian, you've joined a pretty unique club this week. You won two caps on the same day."

I wasn't following, and he could see it.

"Your first and your last," he laughed.

But all that was a long way away when I first caught the rugby bug as an 11-year-old late starter at Llantarnam Comprehensive School.

I'd love to start my story with tales of woe, about how my upbringing was a difficult one, and that everything I've achieved, in life and in sport, was done against all odds.

Alas, this isn't a true underdog story, or a case of a struggle to overcome adversity. In reality, the only struggles I faced in my rugby career were usually brought on by myself, as often as not through a rush of blood to the head; a moment of madness, self-inflicted, whatever you want to call it.

It was only later on that I faced real challenges that weren't of my own making. Health issues for one, and, as I looked to move on from rugby player to, well, whatever comes next, a fight through the legal system to clear my name and protect my reputation.

Having clarified that my story, or at least where it all began, isn't actually that remarkable, now I have to convince you to stick with me as I meander along memory lane. I hope you do as, despite everything, I believe it is a story worth telling.

So then, where does it all start? To begin at the beginning as a far more eloquent Welshman than myself once wrote, well before I plugged my laptop in, well, I was born in Panteg Hospital, Pontypool, on Wednesday, 10 November 1976.

My mum was Sandra. She grew up in the Forest of Dean, with Irish heritage, and her side of the family all still live around the Gloucester area.

That's the Carol side of the family, and that connection allowed both me, and my older brother, to play some rugby for Irish Exiles a bit later in our lives, a first taste of international rugby for me that, seemingly, awoke the Welsh selectors of my suitability.

Mum was married before she met my Dad, and I've got a half-sister and -brother, Jane and Andrew Collins, who are ten and 12 years older than me respectively. They were born in Southall in London, but Mum and her first husband split up while they were still relatively young. Their dad didn't really bother much; he didn't spend a great deal of time with them after getting divorced.

Dad was Malcolm. He was one of eight, born to Iris and Bernard. My grandfather, or Grancha as we used to call him, played for Newport in the 1930s. I've got his caps and medals; they take pride of place in my house. Obviously, he was big into his rugby so I always got on with him and looked up to him when I was a kid.

Dad and his seven siblings grew up in a three-bedroom house in Old Cwmbran. Grancha was pretty old school in his ways and, although you don't notice it at the time, from what I can gather he wasn't very nice to my Nan and his sons didn't like him for that. He was always very good to me though, all the way through my childhood.

Dad met Mum on a Friday night in Cwmbran Workingmen's Club, which, it turns out, was quite the social hub at the time. He was on a night out with Saunders Valve works rugby team. No doubt you can see a rugby theme already materialising in my life and, with hindsight, is there really any wonder that I went down the career path I did?

My formative years were spent in a place called Fairwater in Cwmbran.

It's not a place that left much by the way of memories, as by the time I was three we'd moved to a big council estate called Coed-eva.

What I do know about that first house is that it was rumoured to be haunted.

Mum was always into the spiritual side of things and apparently she would hear things like the stairs going, a cradle rocking – and we didn't have a rocking cradle – rattles going, and things like that.

After asking a few questions, digging around with the locals, they found out that a young baby had died in the house, and with Mum believing in that sort of thing she got a priest to come in and perform an exorcism. It scares the life out of me, if I'm honest!

That was about half a mile away from where we moved when I was three, and I'm assured that the move and the ghost were completely unrelated – it was genuinely just to be in a bigger house.

Our new home was on a road called Stevelee. Again, I apologise that my upbringing didn't provide much by way of drama or social strife, as seems to be the way when you read this kind of book.

Yes, it was a council estate and it would be easy to be critical but the Bronx it wasn't. Thirty-five years on and Mum is still there to this day, which says a lot about the place. It's just a typical sprawling estate, of the kind that cropped up across the UK in the Sixties, and is home to all sorts of families from all sorts of backgrounds.

It was close to where I was soon to start my education at Hollybush Infant and Junior School, and there were plenty of places to find myself as a kid.

We had big woods to play in, there was a hard surface Redgra pitch within 100m of the house, and plenty of fields within wandering distance to get lost in, so if it wasn't the best place in the world it certainly wasn't the worst either, by any stretch of the imagination.

Living opposite us on the estate were two brothers called Darren and Mark Hill. Mark ended up being half of the Artful Dodger, the group who were huge at the end of the Nineties with Craig David. He then went on to be a successful DJ and producer, still is today.

I'm not really in contact with anyone from those early days on the estate these days but I did get in touch with Mark about five or six years ago because we used to play Artful Dodger on the Wales bus on the way to team runs.

The boys would have to take their turn to put a playlist together to entertain everyone so I thought, 'I know someone who can help'.

He said he would but it never materialised, more's the pity. I tried to raise my street cred from non-existent to somewhere, anywhere, above that level, but to no avail.

I wasn't really into playing sport as a young kid. Obviously my Dad loved his rugby and played a lot of lower league stuff, and at the time Andrew was playing football, as he hadn't yet discovered rugby. However, at Hollybush there wasn't a sports minded teacher to really push youngsters that way.

I'd try my hand at football and cricket, because most of my friends were playing, but I wasn't the most dexterous – and that's being kind to myself.

I'd have a go, I'd run around, we'd be playing headers and volleys in the winter and tennis ball cricket in the summer, or a bit of tennis at the local park during Wimbledon fortnight, like everybody else, but I played them all very badly despite my best intentions.

That attitude has stuck with me to this day. I'll have a crack at anything and make no apologies if I'm totally inept!

I've always been pretty close to my Dad but, particularly in the early years, struggled to get on with my Mum. I think that was made worse when they split up, when I was around five years old and Dad moved out.

It was probably inevitable really as I remember I'd be at home with my elder sister, Jane, and the two of them would always be arguing across the top of us. There were a lot of rows going on. That's not a great environment to be in, so I suppose in the long run, it's better for them to go their separate ways.

Dad went back to live in Old Cwmbran with my Nan, Iris. It was only about a mile and a half from Coed-eva so, whenever I'd had a disagreement with my Mum, which was frequently, I'd shoot off over there and either Dad or Nan would have to bring me back.

It was just after my parents split up that I was diagnosed asthmatic, something I've had to live with ever since. I remember I was going into Cwmbran town centre with Dad and we were racing; I ran off ahead and went into my first ever asthma attack. I had to go into a shop where I was given some cold water to drink, to try and calm it down.

At the time there weren't actually that many kids in school with asthma; it was before the dramatic increase in rates documented over the last couple of decades.

I've been on Ventolin ever since, as well as other medication, and all through my career, I've had to manage the issue. I always had to take my medication before training or a match, and I had to ensure that the team physio always had an inhaler in his bag of tricks just in case.

Within about two or three years of my parents splitting up my Dad remarried, to Kim, and they continued living with my grandparents so I'd be there every weekend staying over.

Now, I mentioned that Cwmbran Workingmen's Club must have been the social hub of the time, and here is further evidence. Just as Dad had met Mum there on a Friday night, so he met Kim there on a Friday night.

Clearly there was very little else by way of entertainment or nightlife available in Cwmbran in the Seventies and into the early Eighties.

By the time I was about nine Dad had got a job as a prison officer, and got posted up at a big prison in Evesham, which meant he had to move away. That was pretty tough for me if I'm honest, and I'd find myself going two or three weeks without going across to see him because of shifts etc.

At that age, a couple of weeks seemed a lifetime. It was tough, as I was pretty close to him, like I said, but I didn't have that bond with my Mum.

That went on for a year or two until he managed to get posted back to Cardiff prison and moved back to a house not far from my Nan's.

It wasn't long then before Dad and Kim started a family, so I had two more half-siblings. I'm piggy in the middle as Michelle and Richard are 12 and ten years younger than me respectively, giving a nice symmetry to the family.

Andrew, being that much older than me, became very much the 'in-house' father figure. As Dad wasn't around the house, Andrew was a big influence on me as I grew up. We were typical siblings and we got on well. He and Jane both looked out for me as the baby, but I still got some pastings from time to time.

Skipping ahead many years, Andrew was my first real rugby influence. He played for Newbridge when they were in the top division, captaining them for a year. At Newbridge, he played alongside Andy Allen, a Wales second row who is the father of a teammate of mine at the Ospreys, Morgan Allen.

Anyway, I'd be travelling with my sister-in-law to watch him on a Saturday at places like Neath, Newport, Pontypool, all of the main clubs at the time.

Without a doubt, he was my role model as a youngster hoping to make my way in rugby. I remember he'd take me out running and, on those rare occasions when I'd beat him, he'd take me to the gym and show me up on the weights, just to prove a point.

He also played for Treorchy, when what they called 'the dream' was kicking off, as they threatened to become a leading team in Wales.

He dislocated his knee just before I started to come into senior rugby and had to retire.

His oldest son, my nephew, was in the Dragons age-grade system over the last couple of years and one of his teammates was on the bench alongside me out in Connacht for the first game of the 2014/15 season, a lad called Barney Nightingale.

On his first day of training with the group he was, "Oh, I know your nephew George." Talk about making me feel old. That's a sensation I've experienced a lot in the latter years of my career!

It was after my Dad had moved back to the job in Cardiff that I eventually had a go at rugby. I remember I'd be staying over at his on weekends, and inevitably I'd be sitting around on a Sunday bored stupid, so he said, "Right, I'm not having this, you're going to do something."

That something turned out to be Cwmbran RFC.

The only kit I had was a pair of football shorts and a goalkeeper's top. At that point I'd never really seen any rugby matches, didn't have a clue what I was doing, but I turned up – they were short – and I ended up playing against a club called Cwmfelinfach, up in the Gwent valleys. Right, crack on, son!

My first memory was someone handing me off and I was like, "You can't fucking do that!"

I was completely in at the deep end and, although I wasn't short and stumpy, I wasn't particularly big for an 11-year-old kid.

All my Dad's side of the family were short, they were built to be props. Of the eight, it's only my Uncle Gerald who broke the mould but we're all still in dispute whether he was the gardener's or the milkman's. Come to that, I'm in the same dispute with Dad!

I think the physicality of rugby tended to suit me more naturally than other sports though and after that first hand-off I'd say the game struck a chord with me. I suppose even at 11 I was still late to rugby, kids tend to start at five or six these days.

There were only a handful of games left that season, and by the time the next season arrived my life was transformed as I moved across to Llantarnam Comprehensive where, fortunately, rugby was on the curriculum.

Dad got quite involved with the club and within a year or two ended up being chairman. He's got quite an organisational head on him, to be fair. He enjoys his rugby as well, so it was quite a good combination.

I remember that he'd always organise the end of season tours and we'd always end up in Butlin's. We'd never play any games but the kids would be happy as there'd be plenty to do for the weekend. The dads would be equally as happy to leave us to it so that they could be off at the bar, filling their boots.

Llantarnam Comprehensive was big on sport, unlike at Hollybush.

The Wales legend, Terry Cobner, had been head of PE before I arrived and, by the time I was there, it was a guy called Stuart Harrison, who played rugby for Pontypool and cricket for Glamorgan. His sons also both went on to play for Glamorgan.

My year was the exception, I think, in that the boys were mainly football and we struggled to get a rugby team together. Games would get called off and it was all a bit lacklustre. We were struggling but the year above and below were pretty good which was just typical.

There were actually some pretty sporty guys in the school at that time despite the struggles of the rugby team in my year.

There was a boxer called Gary Lockett, who fought for a world title; he was in my year just a couple of weeks younger than me, and in the year above was a talented footballer called David Gabbidon, whose brother Danny has enjoyed a really successful career with Wales, Cardiff City and West Ham.

Danny was a couple of years younger than me so I didn't really know him, but you could always see he was a bit special. That's quite an impressive sporting alumni for one school over just two or three years.

The rugby team I was playing for probably only ever won something like three or four games all the way through school, and we were on the end of a lot of pumpings over the years.

It was hard going at times but I was always super keen and captained the team regularly. Looking back, I probably annoyed everybody else because I was so keen, I was probably a right pain in the backside.

It didn't go well for the school team but I was still playing for Cwmbran and my game was progressing well. So well, in fact, that by the time I reached Under 14 level I was selected for the Pontypool Schools side.

Although it was a schools representative team, I think that my selection must have been made on the basis of my club rugby; nobody would have selected me if they were only watching Llantarnam if and when we managed to get a team on to the field.

I'd be playing for the club on a Sunday, the school on

Tuesday, and training and playing for Pontypool Schools on a different day so it was all starting to get a bit serious.

By the time I was 15, Cwmbran were beginning to have the same issue as Llantarnam with regards to player numbers, or lack of. I suppose it was indicative of the area really because it was all the same catchment.

As a result I ended up moving to play for Pontypool United. It is a club where my nephew plays now, so it's a bit random going back there after all those years.

I was really, really enjoying my rugby by this stage. I didn't really have a growth spurt until I was around this age so like the rest of the Gough family I played a few games at prop.

By the time I got to Pontypool United though I was reasonably tall, tall enough to be in the back row, and when aged 15 or 16 I shot to six-feet four or five, I moved into the second row to play, where I've stayed ever since.

With all the disappointment of cancellations, and lack of players, at Llantarnam and Cwmbran, I was happy to be somewhere where it was taken a bit more seriously. I used to ride there on my bike for training, it was about eight miles each way, but it was a good standard.

The schools that fed the team, West Mons and St Alban's, were good rugby schools. Because of Pontypool's success over the years, rugby was entrenched in the town and in the schools, and they produced really good players. That was reflected in the opposition as well, the local clubs we'd play against. Everything was up a level on what I'd been used to, but I really enjoyed it.

Just being involved with better players and better coaches helped me to develop. In the winter, the coach, Dai Blake, would come down from Pontypool to pick me up, to save me the 16-mile round trip on my bicycle, and I think that was when, for the first time, I could feel everything starting to come together. It was a good two years.

By the Under 16s, representative rugby changed from Pontypool Schools to Gwent, covering a much wider area.

That was the first time that I really experienced disappointment with rugby.

I got dropped. Nobody told me, it just got put in the paper and I found out in the *Argus*! It was so disappointing; it seemed a really cold way to do it, especially given our age.

For a 16 year old, getting dropped by Gwent Schools was as big a blow as anything I would go on to experience in my career, I can tell you that. How do you handle that when you're still a kid? To this day I'm still waiting for that phone call!

Later in life, I had a similar experience, when I was dropped by Wales in 2009.

I'd been playing regularly for Wales for quite some time at that point, had started four games in the Six Nations and gone on tour to North America, so didn't really anticipate the axe swinging my way.

I was moving house at the time, it was autumn, just ahead of the November internationals, and I had a call off my sister, saying, "Hard lines for not getting selected, I just saw it on the BBC."

That was the first I'd heard of it. I hadn't checked online or anything, but at that stage of your career if you hadn't had the call you just assumed it was business as usual and you'd been selected.

I think about a week later Robin McBryde (Wales forwards coach) rang me up and he was like, "Sorry, I thought someone else had told you," that kind of thing.

I wouldn't say that rugby was my life by the time I'd got to 16, 17, 18, but it was certainly starting to take more and more priority.

I left Llantarnam without really making any kind of impression academically. I was never in any kind of trouble or anything but I got through just doing enough. I passed five GCSEs and started doing my A-levels, but I used to spend all day playing table tennis in the common room at that point.

It wasn't for me and I ended up leaving just after my 17th

birthday, over the Christmas holiday. I was offered work with a guy called Bob Jude. He did ceramic flooring and sponsored Gwent rugby clubs like Pontypool and Ebbw Vale.

It was a real shock to my system, actually having to work hard, real physical tiring stuff, and earning what was, in reality, a pittance I suppose.

I had enough to get by as I was still living at home with Mum. What I did get she was taking half for my keep, so I had about 20 or 30 quid a week to live on. Let's just say I got by!

That lasted about a year. I wasn't enjoying the work and then it reached a point where they started wanting me to work on Saturdays, so it came down to a straight choice of rugby or the job. It was that stark.

For reasons unknown, Pontypool United were beginning to struggle so I went back to Cwmbran, where my Dad was now coaching.

We had a decent enough team but it was less serious than I wanted. I played out the season with Cwmbran but by this point I wanted to be involved somewhere where they took it seriously.

The following pre-season I had contact from a guy called Dale Burn, a fellow Cwmbran lad, a scrum half who'd been at Newport for a year and he sold me the dream of a club who would buy me my boots and pay my taxi fares!

I don't really know where I knew him from but his story is an interesting one. He went on to play more than 100 times for Newport, as well as for Wales A and the Scarlets, but had to retire through injury after a car crash.

He received a big compensation payout but, sadly, ended up getting caught robbing newsagents, pinching fags with his mates.

Before all that, he was the one who convinced me to sign for Newport Youth. It was another step up again for me. There were a lot of the boys who I knew from my Gwent Schools days a few years previously and, right from the start, I felt really comfortable.

I wanted to really have a crack so I focused on making a go of it at Newport.

Rugby was still a year or so away from going professional so, at the time, there was no thought that I could do this for a living. It was just about a desire to play at the highest standard I could and Newport was definitely a step in the right direction.

The coach at Newport was a guy called Steve 'Snickers' Jones. A decent all-round bloke, he was a good coach who got on well with the boys, and he worked with someone called Keith Anderson, who had played for Pontypool.

Keith was one of those types who would always be getting sent off, but he was very charismatic, just a little bit berserk, as I'm sure he'd agree with.

Also at Newport was a young man called Richard Parks. Although he did go on to play for Wales a few times and had a pretty successful career, playing in England and France, he's probably best known for taking on some pretty challenging expeditions post-rugby career, climbing mountains, trekking to the Poles, all sorts of extreme challenges really.

He was always pretty much a man of extremes, even as a 17 year old in youth rugby. He was either on the highest of highs, or the lowest of lows, but he was a very good rugby player and a great person to have at your shoulder.

At that age, probably my big rival was Vernon Cooper, who went on to have a very long career with the Scarlets. He was at Ystradgynlais, and was captain of the Wales Youth team, playing alongside James Griffiths in the second row, so he was blocking my way, if you want.

Whenever Newport played Ystradgynlais we'd go toe-to-toe; we had some real battles. He was a real tough guy, and a warrior, and I'd like to think that the respect between us was, and is, mutual.

Most of my international experience at youth level was confined to the bench thanks to Vernon and James.

My first game for Wales Youth was against New Zealand,

and I remember being gutted that I wasn't starting as it meant I didn't get to face the Haka.

One of the players I was up against that day was someone called Ace Tiatia, and in later years I became very good friends with his brother, Filo, at the Ospreys, a true giant of a man in every way.

Not having a chance to face the Haka is one thing that has stuck with me throughout my career.

I've played against all the European sides, obviously, Australia and South Africa, loads of times.

However, after that youth game I only ever managed one senior Test against New Zealand and it turned out to be the occasion at the Millennium Stadium when they ended up doing the Haka in their changing room, in protest at the WRU's plan of responding to it with a rendition of 'Hymns and Arias'.

Anyway, Dale Burn also convinced another player from Cwmbran to join us as well, a back rower called Richard Stride.

I didn't know Richard before then but he would go on to become one of my best friends. We are still friendly to this day, and I ended up being his best man but, unfortunately, his rugby career was cut very short as he ended up breaking his neck.

He came within a whisker of being paralysed. He came off the pitch and was taken to hospital, no neck brace or anything, where he was X-rayed and the extent of the injury became clear. It was, "Shit, he's hanging on by a thread, literally."

You talk about the life of a rugby player, and I'm not going to grumble, I realise that I've been pretty fortunate to have the career I've had, enjoy so many fantastic experiences and travel to some great places, all thanks to rugby.

Even back then, in my Newport Youth days, I'd made great friends and already enjoyed some times, solely due to my involvement in the game.

Then, when something like that happens you realise how

vulnerable you are and you see a side of rugby that maybe nobody talks about.

Richard wasn't treated very well. He was injured in the February, was paid a little bit of money up until the April, when it was very much, "Thank you very much, now off you go."

His injury meant he could never play again, and although he wasn't paralysed, he did struggle for years, physically and psychologically. Rugby had been everything to him and he's had that snatched away from him.

Things like that do make you question yourself, why you do it, but I suppose there is a risk in everything you do in life.

Why do so many people get up on a Saturday or Sunday, pull their boots on and go out on a cold winter's day to put their bodies on the line with their mates in the name of sport? Some of the so-called extreme sports probably come with less inherent danger than rugby to be fair.

It's a question that seems pretty much in vogue at the moment, when you read article after article relating to concussion, with George North, in particular, being one Welshman suffering more than his fair share of problems.

You can never take away the risk that comes with a contact sport like rugby. What you can do, though, is manage the risk properly and ensure that players are looked after in the best possible way, with decisions made with the player's long-term medical welfare in mind, not the short-term needs of a team or a coach.

Unfortunately, experience tells me that is not always the case.

CHAPTER 2

Taste for adventure

AT THE START of 1995, not long after I'd finished working with Bob Jude, my brother Andrew had friends who were emigrating to Canada and I fancied the sound of it, just doing something different.

I'd already been out there to Toronto, on tour with Pontypool United in 1993, playing five games. Funnily enough, someone recently tweeted me to tell me that a programme from the tour was on Ebay. I ended up spending £30 on it, a crappy effort of a programme to be honest, but I couldn't remember if I had it or not and thought it would be good for the collection.

I flew out to Canada early in the year with a non-returnable, non-changeable return flight booked for the November, about £300 in my pocket and a credit card that my brother had given me for emergencies. There were no plans in place at all; I didn't even have my brother's mate's number.

He was a guy called Kevin Treharne, from Cwmbran.

I'd been told he was picking me up at the airport but as I was disembarking from the plane all that I could think was, 'If this guy doesn't turn up I'm stuck in this airport with not enough money to get home and nowhere to live!'

There was no visa, no job, no plans; I just went out there on a whim, and a promise that Kevin had hooked me up with a rugby club, which turned out to be the Toronto Nomads.

Thankfully, he was waiting for me and I knew that my adventure was on.

Funnily enough as it turns out, close to Ystrad Mynach where I trained with the Dragons in my final season, there's a rugby club called Penallta, and out in Toronto, at the Nomads, was a man from Penallta RFC called Terry Wallace. He had gone into business out there, with Penallta Construction, and I ended up working for him.

I was 17 years old, living in a mice infested house, Penrith Palace, on one of the main streets in downtown Toronto, sleeping on the floor with the mice for company!

There were only a handful of Canadians playing for the Nomads; it was mainly Australians, Kiwis and Brits, all young, single and away from home. It was a great time despite the accommodation.

It's a bit of a cliché, no, it's a huge cliché, but going out there I really didn't have a clue about life. Until that point I'd never had to think for myself or do anything. I had to learn very quickly.

You can compare it to student life I suppose, but we had to train and play, and we had to fit it around work for the construction company, painting, labouring, demolition, plasterboarding. Whatever you could turn your hand to, wherever they needed you.

In reality, I was little more than a dogsbody when I look back, but it was a brilliant experience. Living in the middle of Toronto, my first time in a big city, earning my own money, and the boys were good company.

I was a bit too young to drink legally, the age there was 19, but the Nomads were sponsored by a pub called the Guvnor, and on a Thursday after training that's where we would all head.

They'd put a few bites on for you and we'd have a few beers. Even though they were top division in the Ontario League, the focus was very much on a good social scene. Days at the races, weekends up in ski cabins, it was great.

On a shoestring they ran a firsts, seconds, thirds and fourth team, ladies sides, and it was full of ex-pats, a lot of whom were high up in the banking industry which was huge in the city.

We were working cash in hand but the guys in the team would sort us out with bank accounts and whatever. It really was a great time. I almost didn't come back at the end of the year; it was a very close call.

This was a pretty good era for Canadian rugby too. They'd beaten Wales in Cardiff a year or so earlier, and it seemed a good place to be. Once the Nomads' season was over I convinced myself that I could head back home, play my final season of youth rugby with Newport, and then come back out to Canada.

As is always the way, that wasn't how it played out.

Back at Newport, things were beginning to go very well for me and, with rugby having turned professional a few months prior to me returning to Wales, the thought that, possibly, I could make some kind of living from rugby was starting to dawn on me. It didn't take me long to shelve my plans of heading back to Canada.

Although I was still a youth team player, that season (1995/96) I was involved in training with the senior team quite a few times.

With the youth team, you could get a bit feisty, a bit fiery, because you were up against your peers and, in fact, by that time I would have been one of the older boys.

Stepping up, it was very different. In training I was up against a very experienced gentleman called Kevin Moseley, who famously got sent off playing for Wales against France in the 1990 Five Nations, and I remember him giving me a booting at the first opportunity.

I was nowhere near the ball at the time. It was very much a welcome to senior rugby for me. There was no gently coaxing the youngsters through, it was sink or swim time.

I wouldn't say that I broke immediately into an Olympic-standard breaststroke but I must have made a favourable impression as I started to train with the seniors more regularly, and then, on the final day of the season, I was named on the bench for an away game at Stradey Park, one of the great rugby venues in Wales, against Llanelli.

Richard Goodey was captain, while it was the last Newport appearance for Gareth Rees, a Canadian fly-half who had scored 16 points in his country's previously mentioned win over Wales at the Arms Park, before he headed off to Wasps.

I came on for Mark Workman, and actually played alongside a true Newport legend, David 'Muddy' Waters, on his 702nd and final appearance for the club.

That is still a club record and, looking back, I'm honoured to have shared the pitch with him even if only for ten minutes. He was 40 years old at that point, so he trumps my longevity, playing at the top level beyond my youthful 38!

We actually had a bit of a thumping, losing 56–22, but I did enough to convince the new coaching team of Tommy David, Alun Carter and Steve 'Junna' Jones.

Going into the next season, although rugby was now fully professional, I wasn't contracted as such. I was on appearance money per game, but the turnover over the summer had been huge and we'd seen a lot of players move on. That meant I was thrust into the frontline and was starting most weeks. Good for me financially but not necessarily so great for Newport RFC.

Richard Goodey continued as captain, and he is someone who made a really positive impression on me as a young man.

I compare him to Garin Jenkins when I first went into the senior Wales environment. It can be quite daunting for a youngster to walk into the unforgiving banter of a rugby dressing room, particularly when you don't know anyone, but Richard and Garin both had that knack of making you feel welcome and putting you at ease.

It might be a bit of banter, or some advice in a light-hearted way, but it would put you at ease. It may seem obvious, but I've been in enough changing rooms to know that not everybody works that way.

It's funny because with Wales, when I first got my senior call-up, Garin was the second choice hooker behind Jonathan

Humphreys, who was captain. If Humph didn't know you then he pretty much didn't have any time for you when you came into the group; his focus was entirely on those players in the squad that he knew and trusted, and you had to work hard to earn that trust.

It was the complete opposite to Garin who would always be joking, looking to help newcomers make the transition.

It's not exactly a comic masterpiece, but that's where my nickname came from, from Garin, when I was first called up by Wales in 1998.

He was calling me Van and after a few days I cracked and asked him what Van meant. He just shrugged his shoulders and said, "Van Gough, obviously."

He always had the banter and would make you feel welcome, just like Richard Goodey.

I remember Goodey giving me some nutritional advice one day, that was much needed in all honesty as I was 16-stone soaking wet and needed to add some bulk. His advice? Go out with him to Chepstow every Friday night for a few pints and soak it up with a curry!

By this time I was combining my rugby with an apprenticeship in heating engineering, with a company called Boiler Burner Maintenance, who are still going today, but sooner rather than later I found myself on first-team wages at Newport and I let the apprenticeship slip.

The guy who owns the company, Steve Gooding, lives opposite Richard Stride, so I still see him these days.

I may ask him if he needs me to pick up where I left off, seeing as I'm looking for a new career!

Anyway, it was to prove a tough old season, which was understandable in many ways given that we had lost so much experience during the summer, but I thrived and led the way with 36 appearances.

That was an incredible figure really, not something you can imagine someone getting close to these days, particularly in their first year at senior level.

By the end of the season, the WRU put me on what they termed a National Development Contract and paid me £5,000 a year on top of the match fees I was getting for Newport, which would allow me to go full-time.

Looking back, I wouldn't say it was a stitch-up, but I would say that someone, somewhere, took advantage of a naïve 20 year old.

By that point I was playing A team rugby for Wales, where I should have been receiving a match payment, but it was in the small print of the contract that until any match fees earned passed the £5,000 of the Development Contract, then you wouldn't get any more money.

I actually took it up with the WRU and asked, "Why haven't I been paid?" only to be told, "Read the small print."

There was a harsh life lesson for me there, something I learned from quite quickly. I'm not sure whether I ended up worse off than I would have been, but I certainly would have liked someone to explain fully what I was signing up for.

What contract experience did I have at the time?

But let's be fair, the suggestion that a rugby administrator realised he could pull the wool over a young rugby player's eyes isn't that far-fetched or unbelievable, is it?

It's a bit of a strange one to look back at it, given all the talk these days about central and dual contracts. Sam Warburton wasn't the first player to sign with the Union. Players like Jonathan Humphreys, Derwyn Jones, they were signed up right at the start of the professional era and then there were youngsters like myself on these wonderful Development Contracts.

I don't think there had been any kind of strategic thinking or structure at that point, no real understanding of what professional rugby meant or what it should look like. It was more a case of, "Right, we'd better pay some money to these players then."

Those of us at the club who had contracts, be it national or with Newport, were expected to train full-time.

The thing is, there were only about six or seven of us at the club who had those contracts so full-time didn't necessarily have the meaning you might have expected.

We signed a centre from New Zealand called Paul Cooke, who was an Otago legend, a brilliant guy, very, very funny, but past his best by the time he arrived in Newport it's fair to say.

We would pretend to be professionals, I suppose you could say, doing some old school gym stuff in the day and rugby then on a Monday, Tuesday and Thursday night when the rest of the squad could get in.

The conditioning guy was called Jeremy Moody and it would just be about lifting a bar as many times as you could.

The science behind what we were doing wasn't perhaps at the level that it is today. That's something that you could probably say with real justification across the board in Welsh rugby at the time though, not just at Newport, or at the conditioning techniques in place. It was professionalism in name only.

It took years and years for rugby in Wales to truly become professional in its approach. I hate talking with hindsight but sometimes you have to, and reflecting on what was, for the large part, a black hole really in terms of Welsh rugby success in the Nineties and early Noughties, it's not really surprising.

I think the rest of the world dealt with the transition to professionalism far better that we did here in Wales.

People would try to do what they thought they should, what they understood professionalism was, but it wasn't quite there.

After a tough session with Newport, the club would put on food for us, to ensure we refueled properly they would say, and it was beans, sausage and toast.

Now, that's a great meal, something I love to this day, but I'm not sure what nutritional benefit we were getting, maybe someone reading this can tell me? We tucked in regardless because that was what we were told to do.

The person responsible for catering for us was the son of the kit man and he'd be there stirring the beans with the ladle then slurping on it, "No, that's not quite ready yet," then putting the ladle back in and stirring away again while scratching his head with the dandruff falling in.

You didn't want to look at him preparing it, you were, "Just put it on my plate, I don't want to see how it was made."

When I moved on to play for Pontypridd, the post-training food was usually a whole rotisserie chicken from the supermarket. An improvement, maybe, but, still...

Once the season got underway it was very clear that we weren't good enough and it became a long, hard campaign. Despite some relief in cup competitions, we went the entire season without a win in the league, finishing bottom with the prospect of relegation staring everybody in the face.

On a personal level it was very different.

Despite the club's troubles I'd held down my place in the team, playing 31 times, and I ended up winning Young Player of the Year.

I'd also played for Wales at Under 21 and A team level over the course of the season and was beginning to develop something of a reputation for myself.

As an example of how we were professional in name, but not in reality, here in Wales, I had somehow ended up with a relegation clause in my Newport contract that I'd never asked for.

Clearly it was an admin mistake by one of the guys in the office. Because of the remuneration I was now getting from the WRU as part of my National Development Contract, they had given me a whole new contract instead of just amending the existing one, and in that contract was a relegation clause that hadn't been there previously.

As it was becoming more and more obvious that Newport would get relegated, I advised them that I was going to use this loophole as I felt that, personally, I couldn't afford to drop down a division if I wanted to continue progressing as a player.

At the same time, there were some interesting developments on the international scene for me in the latter part of the season.

As I outlined earlier, I've actually got Irish blood in the family through grandparents, and my brother had represented Irish Exiles when he was playing.

As the name suggests, they are a team for players with Irish connections in England, Scotland and Wales, with a view to identifying potential players who may be able to progress in the green of Ireland.

Anyway, it was during this season that, without me knowing, my Dad had contacted them about me, and I ended up playing for them in a game against Ireland A.

It was within weeks of playing in that game that I got a call from the WRU, inviting me to play for Wales A. Clearly, the appearance for the Exiles had registered somewhere within the bowels of the Union's offices.

So, in March 1998, weeks after playing against Ireland A for the Irish Exiles, I found myself back up against the same opposition, but this time for Wales A.

That game tied me to Wales, ending the Irish connection as swiftly as it had started. As a youngster invited to play for the Exiles I'd never really given it that much thought. I certainly hadn't considered that I may have been going down a route that could have ruled me out for Wales in the future. I just wanted to get out onto the rugby pitch at the highest possible level.

At the time, Wales would have a squad of around 50 training together at Sophia Gardens in Cardiff, so I felt that I was moving in the right direction in terms of my international aspirations, particularly with a tour to South Africa coming up in the summer.

The national coach at the time was a guy called Kevin Bowring, and I recall that he was coming under quite a bit of pressure because of results, including a 60-point thumping against England. With a World Cup the following year, elements of the press were starting to talk about the possibility of him moving on.

By the time the Five Nations ended with a 51–0 loss to France, he decided to take the decision out of the WRU's hands and resigned, leaving Wales without a coach less than two months before heading to Africa.

I remember that while the planning was going on for the tour, there was a memo sent out clearly stating that, on the first day, Swansea coach Mike Ruddock would be addressing the squad.

Now, it must have been pretty close to happening for them to have sent that out – I don't know how close – but three weeks before the tour, the Union opted to put Pontypridd coaches Dennis John and Lyn Howells in charge.

By that stage, I'd formally opened discussions with Ponty about a move there, so having been selected for the tour it suited me down to the ground to have them in charge as I thought, 'Great, we can nail down the contract now.'

As the tour was approaching, it was clear that there wasn't much appetite for the trip among certain senior members of the Welsh squad.

Although we were now three years into the professional era it was probably what you'd call the last of the 'old school' amateur tours.

It was a full month away, a Test against Zimbabwe, three provincial games, another against the Emerging Boks, and a Test against South Africa, the world champions, right at the end of it.

Talk about softening us up in preparation!

Now, it was a tough schedule at any time. With the squad travelling with morale at rock bottom following some pastings in the spring, and the withdrawals mounting day by day, according to the press it was beginning to look something like a suicide mission.

Nevertheless, this was my first time on a Wales tour and, potentially, my first cap, so I was looking forward to it.

In typical Welsh fashion, there was drama before we even left our hotel in Cardiff, with the team almost refusing to travel in a row over money.

The memories around the row are fuzzy to say the least, as I was one of the naïve youngsters who was basically sat there looking on in amazement, but the senior players who were on the trip took exception to changes to the payment schedule that was presented to the squad shortly before departure.

Effectively, I think that with so many withdrawals to the squad, and so many new players travelling, the money men felt that they could downgrade the payments to reflect what they thought was a lesser squad.

The message sent out by the senior players who were on board was unequivocal. We weren't travelling.

It took some hectic renegotiations before hands were shaken and we were on the bus and heading south.

We were always going to be up against it with such a tough schedule, even if we had gone fully loaded, but to go there minus 18 players was tantamount to madness.

Saying that, it was a great tour socially, as I think the adversity brought everyone together.

Our only win came in the first game, against Zimbabwe. It was downhill all the way after that, unfortunately, and unsurprisingly.

I didn't play in that one, but I came off the bench in game two, against the Emerging Boks (lost 13–35) and played against Natal Sharks in game four (lost 23–30).

I was training well, and I thought I'd played well when given an opportunity, but it didn't look as though I was going to get my Test debut.

However, Mark Jones, a tough back rower from Ebbw Vale with a fearsome reputation, had an in-growing hair at the bottom of his back, which was causing him some real problems, and he had to have it removed.

The joke on the tour was that Mark's arse had gone, but in reality, it was an incredibly painful issue.

Whatever, it meant that I got a late call for the game against South Africa, so you can imagine my excitement. What made it even better was my Dad had managed to find out from Dennis, who he was speaking to on my behalf regarding a Ponty contract at the time, that I was starting at the weekend.

He knew before I did and was able to hop onto a flight to ensure he was there in Pretoria for my Test debut.

The week before playing us, we'd watched them beating a very good Ireland team 33–0, so we should have known what was coming.

I was one of six debutants that day. One of the others, Stephen Jones, became an international stalwart for Wales for many years, playing more than 100 times. I went on to win 64 caps. The other four earned 25 between them, with Geraint Lewis winning 16 of them. It was a young, inexperienced team, there was no other way to describe it.

For various reasons, among those missing for this game – who had been involved in the Five Nations just a couple of months earlier – were the likes of Gareth Thomas, Scott Gibbs, Allan Bateman, Neil Jenkins, Rob Howley, Dai Young, Jonathan Humphreys, Gareth Llewellyn, Scott Quinnell and Martyn Williams, to name just some of them. You can see how losing players of that quality would weaken any squad.

We were hopelessly outclassed on the day and conceded 15 tries as we lost 96–13, not surprisingly, a Welsh record defeat.

The song that they played over the PA when they scored a try was 'Tubthumping' by Chumbawumba. I knew that song off by heart by the end of the game.

I remember Dai Llewellyn, the scrum half, coming on for his debut with about ten minutes to go, doing a quick tap and go to speed things up and it was like, "Dai, slow down for Christ's sake, we're 80 points down!"

With hindsight, I bet Dad wished he'd stayed in Wales!

We'd known before the game that we were up against it, but you have to give it your best shot. South Africa coach,

Nick Mallett, branded us "the worst international team he had ever seen".

In reality, I suppose we felt let down by some of those who hadn't travelled. It was never said outright by any player, but the thought was that some had looked at the schedule, building up to a Test at altitude at Loftus Versfeld, and thought, 'Maybe that's a good one to miss.' There may have been a few surgical procedures that summer that weren't necessarily essential at that time, shall we say?

I remember sitting down in the changing room after the game and you had John Davies and Mike Griffiths, two old-school, scrummaging props, with a typical front row mentality. Regardless of the 83-point losing margin, their view was, "Well, we didn't go back in any scrums did we?"

As much as there was disappointment at the time, it was a debut for me and I'll always look back fondly at the day, regardless of how it ended. I was 21 years old playing for Wales in South Africa. What more could I ask for?

I made some good friends on that tour and learned a few things.

Right in the middle of the tour we played Borders in East London, a lovely place between Durban and Port Elizabeth, with waves crashing in, it was idyllic. I didn't play in the game, which we lost quite badly, so when we got back to the hotel after the game, while we were all disappointed, I was looking forward to getting out and experiencing a bit of the local culture. It was my first time in South Africa, after all.

Lyn and Dennis came down to the team room where they delivered the bombshell that nobody was going out tonight, as the performance had been unacceptable.

Some of the Swansea crew tried to challenge that, they were adamant they were going out, but were told if they did, fine, but their return ticket would be at the reception desk for them the next morning and they'd be on their way home.

I was gutted. I hadn't played so it wasn't my fault and I

was in this new place that looked like fun. But, I understood and sloped off to my room to try and get some sleep.

That proved harder than I'd anticipated as all I could hear was music. I tossed and turned all night, getting really frustrated, and not dropping off until well into the next morning.

It was only at breakfast did I find out the truth.

Chris Wyatt, or one-man riot as he was nicknamed, had basically said, "Right, if we can't go out we'll have to bring the party to us" and somehow managed to acquire a karaoke machine.

There were a load of air stewards and stewardesses who had come in off their flights as well, and there was a party in one of the rooms that was still going at four o'clock.

Why didn't anyone think of inviting the 21 year old?

The tour was a bittersweet experience for me. As I explained at the beginning of this book, over the many years since, I've done plenty of interviews or sponsors Q&As, where it always goes:

Q: What has been the high point of your career?

A: Making my first appearance for Wales.

Q: And what was the low point?

A: Making my first appearance for Wales.

Back home in Wales at the end of the tour, I completed the move to Pontypridd almost as soon as we landed, having been able to do most of the negotiations with the caretaker coaches.

Obviously my involvement in that record-breaking game hadn't put them off me!

There was to be a huge twist in the tale over the summer though. Cardiff and Swansea made the decision to break away from the WRU for what was to become known as the 'rebel season', in a bullish attempt to instigate a British & Irish League.

As a result, they were in limbo and found themselves playing a season of friendly matches against English opposition from the Premiership.

35

That obviously meant there was a big hole in the Welsh Premier League that needed filling. In the end, Newport didn't get relegated.

They actually came back to me offering the chance of continuing with the club, right up until the first weekend of the season. They were quite persistent.

The argument they presented was that they hadn't actually been relegated so the clause was null and void and therefore I was contractually bound to them.

I was adamant though; Newport had been relegated. That they had a reprieve at a later date because of what Cardiff and Swansea were doing was irrelevant, they had been relegated and off the back of that I'd made a commitment to Ponty in good faith.

I was already training with Ponty by now, taking a full part in pre-season preparations and I was enjoying it. I liked the ethos of the club and I believed I was making the right move, even turning down the chance to go to Cardiff, who had come in quite late and shown real interest.

There was a hell of a squad in place at the club, players like Dale McIntosh, Dafydd James, Neil Jenkins and Martyn Williams were all established top-level players. They represented what Pontypridd was all about and were the opposite of everything I perceived Cardiff to be, working-class and tough, as opposed to Champagne Charlies, if you want.

I knew within one or two training sessions that it was the right move for me at that point in time.

All the way through my career, every move I've made has been for rugby. It's never been for money. Throughout my career I could have gone to places, or even stayed at places, for more money than I did earn, but it wouldn't have been the best option for Ian Gough, rugby player.

Looking back at my career as a whole, I don't have any regrets about how any of it has played out in terms of rugby.

We'd all like to have earned more money, no doubt, but I'm of the belief that making the right rugby decisions allowed me to maximise my earning potential over the years, so if I missed out on a few pounds here or there, then I believe doing the right thing for rugby reasons saw me make that back down the line.

Chasing the money could have seen me make the wrong choice and I may not have made it to here now to tell the story of a 20-year career as a rugby player. The best example I can give was signing for the Ospreys in 2007.

I would have been on more money staying with the Dragons at that stage, but the decision was about what was best for me as a rugby player, where could I flourish more, be competitive and win things.

There were times during my career when I questioned where I was going, what I was doing. I suppose that is only natural, whatever walk of life you are working in, if you stick at it for as long as I've stuck at being a rugby player.

I had a chance to go to France, to sign for Biarritz, back in 2003, and I was the width of a gnat's cock from going.

I was in the wilderness internationally at that point, after a well-documented falling out with the Wales coach, Steve Hansen, and it was a very tempting offer that I thought long and hard about. Who wouldn't be tempted by life on the French coast? Even a Gwent boy like me could see the attraction.

I ended up staying in Wales with the Dragons though and, honestly, it worked out as the best decision for me. Whether it was intuition or not, it was the decision which worked for me in terms of my long-term career.

As more and more money is coming into the game, particularly in France, I do look at some of the moves and question them. People like Gethin Jenkins, going to Toulon – in his case it was clearly a money decision that was never going to be right for him in terms of his rugby career.

I wouldn't claim to know him particularly well but, knowing what I do about his personality, it was obviously the wrong choice for him as a rugby player.

I don't want to single anyone out, least of all a player like

Gethin who is a true Welsh rugby legend with a CV most players, myself included, could only dream of.

I've seen plenty of moves over the years where the deciding factor was more about money or prestige and not about what would actually be best for them as a rugby player.

At that time, a move to Cardiff would have got me more money but I thought no, the culture, the squad, the environment, everything at Ponty would bring me on as a player.

CHAPTER 3

Piano players
and piano pushers

I MAY HAVE now been a Welsh international, but I was still a few months shy of my 22nd birthday and there was no way I could walk into Ponty as the big 'I am', not that that was ever my kind of behaviour.

The back of the Ponty team bus could be a frightening place, that's for sure.

I found it an incredible place, to sit up the back and listen to the stories that would come out from the likes of the Chief (Dale McIntosh), Andrew Lamerton, Neil Jenkins and Steele Lewis, people I looked up to.

I had no understanding of the hierarchy that was in place and didn't realise that you were supposed to earn the right to sit at the back. All the younger boys would be nudging each other and whispering to each other, "Goughy's at the back of the bus," but none of the senior players ever said anything to me about it.

They must have been thinking to themselves, 'Who's this kid whose just joined us and thinks he can come straight to the back of the bus?' but I was just fascinated by their tales. Mind you, on the way back home when they were having a few beers it was a different scenario and they would terrify the life out of me!

They were trying hard to professionalise things at the club, to do what they thought was right, but it was still quite an old-school set-up.

You had Cenydd Thomas, a club legend, serving as chief executive, signing our cheques at the end of every month but seemingly doing every other job that needed doing as well.

Then there were the Tesco rotisserie chickens after training, followed by Jaffa Cakes, for that vital nutrition!

The key to the success of the club though was the attitude of the guys who were there, and what they represented.

They knew what Pontypridd RFC was all about and what it stood for, and you can never underestimate the value of that in terms of having the right culture at the club.

As many clubs have found out over the years, you can have all the talent in the world available, but if the culture is wrong, if you haven't got a 'team', then the talent on its own won't get you to where you want to be.

The highlight of that first season was a run to the last eight of the Heineken Cup but, in truth, we scraped through.

We were in a pool with Glasgow, the Italian side Treviso, and Colomiers from France. We got off to a winning start in Scotland and then beat Colomiers at our Sardis Road ground, 32–27, on a great afternoon for the club.

Disappointingly, we followed that up with three straight defeats, the third coming in Italy away to Treviso at Halloween.

We found ourselves in a bar after the game, with the usual shenanigans going on. I think a few fire extinguishers went off, while some of the senior boys were dissecting the performance over a beer or two.

Discussions were starting to get a bit heated, and I remember Dale McIntosh coming across to calm people down, "Come on guys, what's happening, let's have another beer," that kind of thing. Steele Lewis reacted, told him to bugger off, or words to that effect, receiving an open hander across the face for his troubles.

That was it, Steele was up, asking the Chief outside, Steele's brother Jason was behind him, and I remember them marching towards the door, which swung open and a great big Maori fist came through, spread-eagling Steele.

The paramedics were on the spot quite quickly, and Steele wasn't in a great way, while I was standing there, open-mouthed, trying to comprehend what had just happened.

One of my teammates was laid out, seeing stars, by another teammate.

He was eventually brought around, by which time we had to get back to the hotel as we had an early morning flight and were leaving the hotel at 5 a.m.

Everyone emptied their mini-bars for the journey home, I got on the bus and at the back, not three hours after Steele had almost been killed by Dale, they were sat with arms around each other, having a singsong and finishing off the contents of their mini-bars!

Clearly my confusion was written all over my face as Steele asked what was wrong, and I said, "He nearly killed you a couple of hours ago," to which Dale piped up, "Don't worry bro, we do this all the time!"

The thought, 'What the hell am I doing here?' did cross my mind at that point!

The following week we thumped Glasgow at home and despite what has to be described as an average record of three wins and three defeats, we managed to finish second in our group, the reward for which was the daunting away trip to Paris where we faced French giants, Stade Français, in the quarter-finals.

It's fair to say that few people expected a side that had lost twice to Treviso in the group stages to cause the French champions much concern. A comfortable home win was predicted and, despite our best intentions, that's the way it played out.

We were on the wrong end of a 71–14 scoreline. I'd like to be able to say that Stade scored from nine lucky breaks but I'd be lying!

They were on fire that day. It was a typically French

performance, when they hit form they were unplayable. We went with a good team on paper, people like Kevin Morgan, Daf James, Neil Jenkins, Martyn Williams, Chief, but we just couldn't live with them and were chasing shadows all game.

I would go on to play in three more Heineken Cup quarter-finals, with the Ospreys, and would lose each time.

Following my involvement in South Africa, my international aspirations had pretty much stalled, to be honest.

Graham Henry, a Super Rugby winning coach from New Zealand, had been installed as Bowring's permanent successor following the South Africa debacle and results were improving.

All those who had missed that tour were back in and, to my frustration, I found my involvement with the national squad limited to just a couple of A team games and one game in the 1999 Six Nations, away to Scotland.

That was a game most notable for Scotland winger John Leslie scoring their first try after only about five seconds, robbing Shane Howarth to win the kick-off and going straight through to score a super-quick try – the quickest I've ever seen at that level to this day.

I still had aspirations of being involved in the World Cup later that year, which was being held in Wales, but I was very much on the fringes of the squad as the tournament drew closer.

I was sounded out about my availability for the summer tour to Argentina, which was a huge boost as it meant I was still in the frame. However, in a game against Neath in March I discovered that Dave Tiueti's head was tougher than my arm, and the resulting fracture meant that I couldn't go.

Gareth Llewellyn was called up for the tour in my place, having not played for Wales in 18 months, since the Five Nations in 1998, just prior to the disastrous South Africa tour, as it happens. He did well in back-to-back wins in Argentina, and he then went to the World Cup while I missed out. One thing I've learned about professional rugby is that selection at the top level can be as much about fortune as anything else. On this occasion, Gareth's fortune was my misfortune.

At the end of that season I remember going away on holiday to Mexico, with my partner at the time, and every time I phoned home there was an update that somebody had left Ponty.

We'd failed to qualify for the Heineken Cup for the coming season and, financially, I think that hit the club in terms of its ability to pay wages and other outgoings.

The coaches, Dennis and Lyn, paid the price. They were kind of victims of player power, for want of a better phrase. They'd been there a long time, and there were a lot of senior, established players, who carried a lot of sway within the club and maybe felt that they were no longer the right people to carry it forward.

There were players moving on as well, people like Martyn Williams and Neil Jenkins. There were about six in all, key players, who had either retired or moved on to pastures new, seemingly all heading down the well-worn path which is the A470 to Cardiff, a route for players from Ponty to the Arms Park for many years.

Given the historically strong rugby links between Ponty and Cardiff, I find it ironic that so much fuss was made following the introduction of regional rugby in 2003 and the failure of the Celtic Warriors, the region formed between Ponty and Bridgend, just a year later.

It meant that in 2004, Ponty came under the Cardiff Blues umbrella – but because of the strength of feelings against the merger among Ponty fans, it was never going to be an easy transition despite the obvious long-term connections between the two clubs. Eleven years later, that collaboration is still struggling in many ways, despite the rugby side of things being stronger than ever.

In any event, things remained positive with Richie Collins,

a real club legend, coming in to take over the coaching along with Steele Lewis, while at the same time there were exciting youngsters like Rob Sidoli, Ceri Sweeney and Johnny Bryant.

Ceri, in particular, was quite a tenacious character, and he still is. I remember when he first started to be involved around the first team, he turned up for training on a Monday with a black eye, which hadn't occurred on the pitch. There was a lot of questioning, and eventually, it came out that he'd upset the head of the supporters' committee.

We had a cup match up in Cwmllynfell, up in the Swansea Valley, the following week. I wasn't playing but had gone along to support the team, with Neil Jenkins and Ceri.

We were watching the game when a pint of something comes flying past my eyes, just misses Neil, and explodes against the wall soaking him. We turn around and it's the woman who was head of the supporters, who is saying, "Sorry, Neil, it wasn't meant for you, it was for Sweeney."

He was stood there looking very sheepish, he would still only have been 18. It turned out that, apparently, he had been using profanities in the clubhouse, which she had objected to. He told her to "Fuck off, this is a fucking rugby club and if you don't like it then fuck off," and paid the price for it!

Another youngster coming through was Michael Owen, and I remember him at 18 years old telling me quite earnestly over lunch one day that although I lacked ability, I tried really hard.

I think by this time I'd had four or five senior caps and was in the best form of my career. Cheers, Mike!

I reminded him about that conversation four or five years later, by which time he was my captain at the Dragons and on his way to becoming a Grand Slam winning captain and a British Lion.

In fairness though, Steve Jones used to make it quite clear to us at Newport who were the piano players and who were the piano pushers. There's a need for both. After all, you've got to get the piano on stage and set up in the right place and at the right time if the star of the show is going to be able to perform.

To continue with the metaphors, I'm under no illusions that I'm certainly a man handler, not a ball handler, when it comes to rugby.

The longer you do something, the more you understand what your niche is and know your limitations. I'm comfortable that I've enjoyed a lengthy career, longer than most, despite lacking ability, as Mike had told me back in 2000.

Gethin Jenkins was another one just starting off. He was a smiley little kid, a really happy one, he's just turned into a miserable so-and-so as he's got older!

He was in terrible shape, but he had great skills. He worked in McDonald's in Talbot Green and I remember speaking to Garin Jenkins, the Swansea hooker, on one occasion after a Wales training session.

He told me that he was off to Talbot Green on the way home. When I asked why his response was that 'Melon Head', as Gethin was known, was working.

I still didn't get it, and he replied, "Well, you go up and ask for a McChicken sandwich and he gives you three bags of food. The family are eating for a couple of quid."

He'd be filling you up, winking and smiling at you, and there'd be a constant stream of rugby players calling in on their way home!

It's funny to remember Gethin like that as he has had an incredible career and is certainly one of the best Welsh players of all time.

I was also reunited with my old mate Richie Parks, and we still had a good core of players there as we entered into the new Welsh Scottish League, Glasgow and Edinburgh coming on board in what was to be a forerunner of the Celtic League, as Welsh rugby continued to wrestle with professionalism.

Probably our favourite away trip was always Dunvant, not some of the more glamorous destinations.

The reason?

They always had the best-looking barmaids who were employed from Swansea University!

The club certainly got it right, because with an afternoon kick-off, the visiting team and supporters would end up staying, watching the televised game on S4C at 5.30, and drink into the night. That was the away game that every Welsh team would look forward to!

Ebbw Vale was always a tough place to go to. It always seemed to be minus two Celsius, even in the summer. They had a passionate crowd, and a really tough, formidable, core of a team built around people like Kingsley Jones and Byron Hayward, the kind of people that you would follow into the trenches.

It was up there that I had a scrap with a certain Kuli Faletau, father of Toby.

That makes me feel really old, just thinking about it.

Kuli must have been about 40 by then, regardless of what his passport will tell you. He'd caught me at the lineout and we were grappling with each other, when Mark Jones, he of the in-growing hair in South Africa, sent through the biggest right hook I received in my whole career.

When I got up five minutes later I was asking what number my bus was!

My nose was across my face and my eye was split. I couldn't see out of it for about a week and a half. I've carried the scars of that one ever since, as I was left with a droopy right eye to this day.

It was a bit of a cheap shot from behind but I've toured with Mark, he's a funny bloke, and there's no hard feeling.

I still see him with his family at the Glamorgan Health Club in Llandarcy. Kingsley has some gags about Mark in his repertoire, mostly revolving around his stammer. I think there are only a handful who could get away with that, I know I certainly wouldn't do it!

On a personal level, I had finally seemed to make the breakthrough with Wales. Having missed the World Cup the previous autumn, due to my broken arm, I had been brought into the squad for the 2000 Six Nations, featuring in all five games.

It was a campaign that turned into a strange one, to say the least.

On the field, with three wins and two losses, it wasn't a bad campaign, particularly in comparison to the usual late Nineties form.

However, midway through the competition, what is now known as the 'Grannygate' scandal broke. It came out that Shane Howarth and Brett Sinkinson, two players that Henry had brought over with him from New Zealand and apparently eligible to play for Wales through the grandparent rule, didn't actually have any Welsh parentage at all.

Therefore, they weren't qualified to play for Wales.

Despite this, Howarth, a full back who had previously played for the All Blacks, had won 19 Welsh caps, while flanker Sinkinson, had played in the red of Wales 14 times.

The news broke just a few days after we had lost to England at Twickenham, a game where both of them had started and I came off the bench.

A Scottish newspaper had carried out an investigation and uncovered the truth. As the IRB (rugby's world governing body) investigated themselves, it became clear that all sorts of people in authority were complicit – mainly because of an absolute lack of checking the facts.

It seemed as though both the WRU and the IRB had simply taken the players' word for it without asking to see proof.

Reflecting on it today, as a Welshman and someone proud to have worn that red jersey 64 times, the only words I can use to describe the whole farce really are "piss take".

There were obviously people in a position who knew what the score was but they chose not to act for whatever reason.

I feel for people like Kevin Morgan, who I had been playing

with at Ponty and who I would then play with at the Dragons. He is a great lad and a very good player, who wore his heart on his sleeve in everything he did, and he had to watch someone like Shane coming in, with absolutely no Welsh qualifications at all, and take his shirt.

Don't get me wrong, I think Shane was a great player, as was Brett for that matter, but he robbed Kev of the chance to pass the landmark of 50 caps, which would have been a special achievement he could have been proud of.

Putting aside any views on foreign players being allowed to qualify through residency, which is always an emotive subject, and one that saw me get into trouble a few years later, this was just wrong, a scandal.

Both Shane and Brett stayed around in Wales to their credit, they didn't just head off home. I went on to play with Shane for three years at Newport and really got to know him, seeing just what a great player he really was.

Brett went on to qualify for Wales legitimately through residency and actually played another six times for the country. It was different for Shane though, as they tightened up eligibility criteria off the back of this incident and stopped players who had already been capped by one country from switching allegiance.

It was too late, however, for those who had lost out on international caps and, of course, the financial benefits that come with that, because of the fraudulent behaviour of others.

CHAPTER 4

My big mouth

IN THE SUMMER of 2000 I was coming out of contract once again, and it was time to take stock of what I wanted next.

I'd had a great experience with Pontypridd, but the second season had been a disappointing one.

My time at Ponty wasn't maybe the greatest two years in the history of the club but I hold dear my time at Sardis Road. It was a great club with strong values, which really knew what it stood for.

I did feel really disappointed about what was to happen to Ponty a few years later in 2003/04.

In truth, it was a really difficult period for all rugby clubs in Wales; it's probably fair to say that the transition to professionalism, still in its infancy when I was a Ponty player, had pretty much failed. The Welsh clubs were trailing behind the rest of Europe – however you wanted to measure it – and it was clear that something had to happen.

Like I touched on previously, the Ponty/Cardiff fit seemed to make absolute sense to me but, when regional rugby came into being in 2003, the club was put together with Bridgend to form the Celtic Warriors. It was never a match made in heaven.

It was a shame that the change to regional rugby coincided with the period when the guys backing Ponty – the Just Rentals/Buy as You View people – just couldn't make the financial commitment required at the time. Leighton Samuel at Bridgend could, and the balance of power in the relationship wasn't an equal one, leading to a pretty rapid falling apart of the partnership.

GOUGHY: A TOUGH LOCK TO CRACK

Within a year, the Warriors were gone, and Cardiff belatedly became Pontypridd's region. I believe that if the money had been there at the time, a Rhondda Cynon Taf region, separate from Cardiff Blues, could have been a strong entity; one that would have survived and gone on to do really well.

I wasn't involved with the Warriors but a lot of good friends were, and that was the first time that I'd seen what could be called the tough end of professional sport.

I think there's too much water passed under the bridge for Ponty now, in terms of the elite end of professional rugby.

The game has continued to move on and I think it's impossible to build a successful top-tier club now away from the main population centres, where the sources of revenue are based, be that supporters to buy tickets, commercial partners and sponsors, whatever. Money now makes rugby tick over and the reality is, in huge swathes of Wales, away from the population centres, there is no money. It's as harsh as that. The four existing regions have found out for themselves how tough it is to survive and they can turn to far larger populations and commercial bases than a side like Ponty – or any Valleys team – could aspire to in this day and age.

Unfortunately, unless someone came in with real money, and you're talking millions and millions available to pump in every season for many years, I think the chances of that happening have long passed.

That is such a shame because I don't think many teams have ever fancied their chances of going up into the Valleys and going toe-to-toe with the tough, hard-edged kids that get produced on the rugby pitches up there; kids who haven't had everything handed to them on a plate.

It's been a tough ask, since Cardiff took responsibility for the north side of the M4 there, to mix what Ponty have always stood for, with the perception of the big city slickers from Cardiff. I've mentioned the traditional club links, but I think after the demise of the Warriors, for those at the Ponty end of the A470 it was a case of once bitten, twice shy. They've worked hard at it and things are improving as far as the relationship between Cardiff and Ponty goes, but, for me, it's definitely a "what if?"

Back at Newport, in the two years since I'd moved to Ponty, there'd been a real transformation.

The 1998/99 season had again seen the team struggle for any kind of form, the club finishing bottom but one in the league following the 'non-relegation' the previous year.

However, one important development had seen the club transformed off the field.

There was a forward thinking new chief executive, Tony Brown, who'd brought money and contacts with him and, in little more than a year, they had turned it around.

A best ever league finish in 1999/2000 meant Newport had qualified for their first ever Heineken Cup, and a recruitment campaign had seen real quality added to the squad.

People like Shane Howarth, Peter Rogers, Fiji captain Simon Raiwalui and, most notably of all, ex-Springboks captain Gary Teichmann, had been brought in and there was a real buzz about the place.

It wasn't just the rugby, it was also what they were doing off the pitch that attracted me, the innovative community and commercial stuff. In Wales they were truly ahead of the game, doing things that no other club were and that was reflected in the way crowds had exploded at Rodney Parade.

Some of the innovative community work, the commercial work, that the club was doing at the time was so far ahead of the rest, that there aren't many around operating at that level now. The end result was regular crowds in the 10,000 bracket and, to be honest, as a local boy who had come through at the club a few years earlier, when I received the call to rejoin the club, it didn't really take much time to make my mind up.

It was a really attractive proposition and I was excited about going home.

That first season was a pretty positive one, although the team failed to match the second-place finish of the previous year, finishing fourth.

The club's first Heineken Cup campaign saw memorable wins over Bath and Castres but we couldn't account for Munster. That left the Principality Cup, which was undoubtedly the highlight of the season.

For some reason now lost in the sands of time, I didn't play in the cup run, despite making 27 appearances that season prior to the final. It was a good run by the team with some impressive performances and big wins against the likes of Aberavon and Dunvant, before Ebbw Vale were seen off in the semi-final.

That meant we were set for a big day out at the Millennium Stadium in Cardiff for the final, against Neath. Cup final day in Cardiff was the traditional season ender, when supporters could enjoy a big day out at the home of Welsh rugby and where club men – good, loyal rugby people – would get the chance to play at the national stadium.

There was a crowd of over 37,000 present for our game against Neath on Sunday, 13 May 2001; it was a really special occasion. The Neath side was packed with quality, experienced players like Brett Sinkinson, Rowland Phillips and Mefin Davies, as well as young talent like Duncan Jones and Shane Williams, who would go on to have such distinguished careers.

They were a good side and we knew that it was going to be a tough day at the office.

As expected, it was a close game and was tied at 3–3 at half-time, before we managed to pull ahead thanks to a try from Adrian Garvey and a couple of kicks from Shane Howarth. If we thought that was it we had to think again as, in their usual dogged way, Neath threw everything at us and a try from Kevin James, brother of Wales and Ospreys prop, Paul, meant it was a tight finish. Shane dropped a late goal for us to ensure we won 13–8.

It was only Newport's second ever cup win so it was clearly a huge achievement.

About three-quarters of the way through the game I dislocated my shoulder going into a ruck, and I remember lying on the floor holding my arm in real pain, only to hear one sole voice clearly over the din of the big cup final crowd, a Neath supporter shouting, "For God's sake, Gough, get up. There's nothing wrong with you!"

For about ten or 15 minutes I was in the changing room with the physio trying to get the shoulder to pop back in – without any luck, as I couldn't relax enough. They told me that I was going to have to go to hospital to have it put back in.

I was watching the game on a television screen in the room and I'd just seen the drop goal going over that had ensured the win and I was most concerned by this news.

"If I go into hospital, it doesn't mean that I'm going to miss the after-match does it?" I asked, thinking about the celebrations.

The response was what I didn't want to hear – if I went into hospital I would be under general anaesthetic to have it done and would be kept in overnight.

"Well, you'd better give it another go then," was my response to that!

In an example of mind over matter, I made sure I relaxed enough and, just about as the final whistle was going, my shoulder popped back into the joint. I wouldn't need that ambulance after all.

I managed to get out onto the field to celebrate with the team and I shed more than a few tears, which I'll put down to all the gas and air I'd had while they were trying to sort the shoulder out!

The best thing about it was that because of the injury I actually beat the rest of the team back to Rodney Parade after the game!

They stopped off at a pub called the Coach and Horses in St Mellons in Cardiff, a regular refreshment point for us on the way back from away games, while I was in fact taken to hospital for an X-ray before heading to our ground to meet up with everyone.

I got there about ten minutes prior to the team bus, so you can imagine the welcome I received off the supporters who were all there waiting to cheer us home. I think they almost cheered themselves out on me. I certainly milked it for all I could.

Yes, there were some big name imports in that side, people like Garvey, Howarth, Teichmann and Andy Marinos, but there was a core of local boys who had come up through the ranks at the club. Not just me, boys like Dale Burns, who got me to Newport as a teenager, Jason Forster, Alix Popham, local boys who were part of what was becoming a thriving club, on and off the field. At this point, the future for Newport RFC was looking positive.

It was a special day for the club, and for me personally. It was my first silverware, and the club's first in quite a few years as well. It's one of the big highlights of my career, being a local boy, and I've still got that jersey, signed by the team. It's one I'll always cherish.

That summer was a Lions tour, with Graham Henry in charge for the trip to Australia. I had initially been included on a short-list, which was presumably not that short, as reality soon hit in.

First of all it became clear that I wouldn't be going to Oz; instead I was penciled in for Wales' trip to Japan, only for the shoulder injury sustained in the final at the end of May to rule me out of that one as well.

That meant I had the summer to prepare for what promised to be another exciting season at Rodney Parade.

For an all too small period of time, Newport were really up there at the top of the game in Wales.

The 2001/02 season, with Ian McIntosh, a former coach of South Africa, in charge, saw us record some impressive victories in the Heineken Cup, including a win over French champions Toulouse, but our fate was sealed in a game against Leinster at a packed Rodney Parade.

I was named on the bench, and came on for the last half-hour instead of Mike Voyle. We led by just a point with just under ten minutes to go, and had just been awarded a kickable penalty that would have taken the score to 24–20.

At that point, the lights went out on us, literally. A floodlight failure meant that we had to come off the pitch and there was a delay that must have been 15 minutes long.

I remember that they didn't want to come back out, but when they eventually did, for some reason, we ran the penalty instead of taking the points, failed to make it count, and lost the momentum. Leinster scored two late penalties to win the game.

Ultimately, we were disappointed in the league as well, despite being odds-on for the title at one point. We were leading the table going into mid April, only to lose consecutive home games to Neath and Cardiff, with a thumping away to Swansea in between.

We won our last three games to put us back top of the table, waiting on the outcome of Llanelli's game away to Cardiff. The Scarlets needed to win at the Arms Park and Cardiff were unbeaten at home all season. With about half an hour to go, Cardiff were well in front, but Llanelli threw everything at them and were 25-all with time up, when Stephen Jones put over a penalty to win the game, and the title.

Fair play to them, it was a great achievement, but talk about gutted! A second second-place finish in three years seemed scant consolation for our efforts.

Regardless, there still seemed plenty to be optimistic about looking into the coming season, with Springbok legend Percy Montgomery signing, although there was another change of coach, the former England scrum half Richard Hill taking over, with Leigh Jones coming in from Ebbw Vale.

I caught up with Ian McIntosh again in November 2014,

when he was over to see South Africa on their tour, and it reminded me what a great coach he was.

He was possibly the most charismatic coach I ever worked with, he had a way of inspiring people and really making you believe in him, what he was doing, and what he wanted you to do.

It's a bit of a catch-22 situation though, as even though we had great success in that season and were a whisker away from winning the league, his health wasn't good and he went home after a year.

Given that Allan Lewis, the coach who had re-signed me, had moved on before him, then a year later we had Richard coming in, it was three coaches within as many seasons and that is just too much turnover for any team to not only remain consistent but to improve year on year.

Although Richard is a good coach, it wasn't quite the same. Whereas Mac was a world-class coach and, like I said, had real charisma, commanding respect from his players, Richard was following in difficult footsteps and he never quite clicked.

Leigh found it difficult coming into a different environment. I think he worked well with the senior players at Ebbw, the guys like Mark, Byron and Kingsley, who he had worked with for years, people who controlled the team environment, and he fed in through them.

Coming into Newport with some incredibly strong personalities in the environment, like Shane Howarth, Percy Montgomery, people who had been there and done it all and had strong opinions on the game, both Richard and Leigh had a tough time filling Mac's shoes.

It's fair to say that we struggled that year.

What absolutely nobody realised at the time, even though we got to another Welsh Cup final in May 2003, which we lost heavily to Llanelli, was that this was as good as it got for Newport RFC.

I suppose it's what you call the winds of change, but Welsh rugby politics meant that 2002/03 was to be the final season of the club operating at the top table, with the WRU instigating the switch to regional rugby.

I do feel that it's such a shame that the hard work of so many people at Newport RFC during that period eventually counted for very little in the long-term.

There was a lot of effort and investment for what were two or three modestly successful years on the field, but the real story had been the incredible growth off it, which should have been the platform for the club to really establish itself at the top table for many more years.

That last season pre-regional rugby, players realised there were troubles but you tend not to get too caught up in the politics, you let other people worry about that and just get on with the rugby.

The regional revolution, for want of a better term, was about pooling resources to make teams more competitive at the top end of the game, and to make Welsh rugby more cost effective.

There were going to be five regions representing Wales at the top table, with some mergers taking place between leading clubs. Celtic Warriors saw Bridgend and Ponty coming together, the Ospreys were Neath and Swansea, while Gwent was going to be a combination of Ebbw Vale and Newport, with Llanelli and Cardiff standing alone.

It was never going to be easy bringing together players, staff and supporters from rival clubs, but what choice did we have? Like I said, we would let other people do the worrying and just get on with the rugby.

While all the changes were going on around the regional restructure I, along with most of the senior players in Wales, were focusing not on that, but on the impending Rugby World Cup.

After missing the Japan tour in the summer of 2001, I had regained my place in the squad that autumn, featuring twice before the turn of the year.

I was then involved as a replacement for the opening game of the 2002 Six Nations, an absolute thumping in Ireland, a record 54–10, after which Henry immediately resigned.

His forwards coach, Steve Hansen, stepped in to take over, initially on a caretaker basis, before being confirmed as permanent, even before the end of the competition. Losses to Scotland, France and England (the second 50-point hammering of the spring) were clearly enough to impress the WRU blazers!

Graham was quite a dominant character, but a nice guy, and his record with the All Blacks after leaving Wales has underlined what a quality coach he is.

It actually came as quite a shock to us as players at the time but, I think he had tried to change things over the last year or so of his time in charge and struggled to get the response he wanted, in terms of both performance and results.

As well as Hansen, another person around at that time was Scott Johnson, an Australian skills coach who had been brought in during the last days of Henry's regime.

Reflecting on my time in the game, Welsh rugby permanently seemed to be in a state of transition; it was always top of the world or in the depths of a crisis, and at this point, as Steve took over from Graham, again, it seemed like a crisis to many people.

I think that's the Welsh way. We are such an emotional people there is never a middle ground, it seems like we get bored as a race if everything is just OK.

OK doesn't give you the crest of a wave or the depths of despair, OK doesn't let you experience the wonderful, contradictory emotions that have become synonymous for Welsh people with the fluctuating form of its rugby team.

We can all remember the high points of Grand Slams and whatever, but I can recall being in Edinburgh Airport after a loss in Scotland and seeing supporters turning their backs on the team in disgust.

Or there was the time we lost in Italy after confusion at the end with referee Chris White about whether there was time for us to go for a lineout to win it after he had awarded a penalty in the final minute. We were three points behind so if we'd gone for the points we could have drawn the game, but he advised us we had time to go for the lineout to try and win the game, only to blow the final whistle when James Hook put the ball into the corner. Instead of playing the lineout as expected, his whistle went and we'd lost 23–20.

As the bus was leaving the stadium after the game there were supporters outside waving at us – only, when you looked closely you realised they weren't waving, they were making wanker signs at us!

There was another game in Italy where Colin Charvis had the nerve to smile while we were losing and Wales' 'national' newspaper ended up labeling him the second most hated man in Wales, behind only Saddam Hussein. I mean, come on!

I think that extreme reaction is fuelled by the press, who never seem to find a consistent middle ground. Again, reflecting what I said about the Welsh psyche, run of the mill doesn't sell papers, does it?

Mind you, does anything sell newspapers these days? As circulations plummet then the heights become ever higher and the depths ever lower to try and stir emotions and generate sales.

Anyway, ultimately, I missed out on the 30-man squad that Steve Hansen selected to go to Australia for the 2003 Rugby World Cup and, because of that, I ended up learning the hard way about what you say to the press when in a certain frame of mind!

Robin Davey, the long-standing rugby writer at the *South Wales Argus*, is a good guy, a passionate supporter and advocate of Gwent rugby in all its forms.

He also has an impeccable sense of timing.

I'd just been told by Steve that I hadn't made the cut, and that he was taking Brent Cockbain instead of me.

Brent was a lock from New South Wales, who had played

youth and Under 21 rugby for Australia. His brother, Matt, played more than 60 times for the senior Australia team.

He had been in the UK for four years having original signed for London Irish, moving to Pontypridd a year later in 2000, where he had spent the last three years, qualifying for Wales on residency in the summer of 2003.

He actually qualified just in time to be selected for the World Cup warm-up game against Romania at the end of August, just three or four days before Steve had to name his final selection.

I lined up alongside Brent in the second row for that match, a game that we won comfortably, 54–8. I thought I'd played quite well, after training well all summer, while Brent hadn't trained that much because he'd had a few injuries.

At the selection meeting with Steve a few days later, he told me that I wasn't in the squad. He said that I was an inch too short to play second row for Wales at that time. Brent was an inch and a half taller than me so that counted against me.

I was absolutely gutted.

I'd realised I was down the pecking order and there were a few players in front of me. I'd have been mad not to see that, given I'd not been involved for over a year prior to the Romania game. But I found this a very bitter pill to swallow, particularly the reason I'd been given.

How could I change things? What could I work on? If I went away and stretched myself on a rack, to get that extra inch, would I then be suitable to play for Wales?

As I left the meeting my phone went and it was Robin.

It was pure chance, but talk about timing. I get on very well with him, always have done, and he has an impressive nose for a story. He got me as I was walking out of the barn at the Vale Hotel, where Wales are based when in camp, just after I'd been told that I wasn't going to the World Cup, the second one that I'd missed.

The first, a broken arm, well you can accept that, but missing out because you're a couple of inches shorter than an

Australian whose residency qualification had come through that week?

The old saying is 'loose lips sink ships'. You can say things in the heat of the moment that have a huge impact on your life and you live to regret it. I let Robin have everything he wanted, and more.

"I've been stabbed in the back," was the line that stood out.

I even had a chance to retract it.

In fairness to Robin, he had gone straight to Jim McCreedy, the team manager at Newport, who had said to him, "You'd better not print that," so Robin rang me back to ask if I wanted to retract my comments.

No, I told him, it was fine, I stood by my comments. I was on my high horse and that's what I wanted to say. I was being stubborn, wanted to make my point, and Robin went ahead and printed it.

The end result was it cost me nigh on two years in the international wilderness. I didn't play for Wales again until 2005 when Steve was long gone back to New Zealand.

It was a harsh lesson for me to learn.

I remember years later, having chats with Richard Hibbard at the Ospreys, when he was having big clashes with Robin McBryde (Wales forwards coach from 2006 onwards).

I had to pass on my own experience, explaining that you have to learn to sometimes keep your head down and your mouth shut, and avoid the crossfire coming over the top.

It might seem a good idea at the time, to vent your feelings, but it can prove costly. That's a piece of advice that I've passed on many times since and I'll stand by it whatever walk of life I go into now that my rugby playing days are behind me.

As much as I achieved what I wanted at the time and got my feelings out there in the public domain, the effect was that I was on the outside looking in for quite some time afterwards.

As a result, I almost ended up going to France, to play for Biarritz, an opportunity I mentioned previously.

Because of the publicity, I think, an agent got in touch with the offer and I was right on the verge of doing it, I was going to get away from Wales and all the crap, as I thought it was.

In the end I didn't go through with it because I realised I was doing it for all the wrong reasons.

As I said earlier, every move I've made as a rugby player has been for rugby reasons and that wouldn't have been the case this time. I would have been running away from the problem and that's not me.

I stayed and was ready to have a crack at it with the new region.

So, instead of boarding a plane to Australia or Biarritz, I headed back to Rodney Parade, where Mike Ruddock, a successful former Swansea coach, had been put in charge of the new team called the Gwent Dragons, soon to become the Newport Gwent Dragons.

All credit to him, in the face of adversity and plenty of resistance in the boardroom and in the stands, we had a very good season.

It was a strange transition. Even today, I speak to people, ex-Newport supporters, who will tell me that they gave up watching rugby at that time because they were so disillusioned with what happened.

My personal opinion, then and now, is that it should have stayed as clubs, albeit super clubs as the ones best placed to compete.

That's what we've got to this day at Llanelli and Cardiff anyway and, for whatever reasons, the wider Gwent public hasn't bought into regional rugby.

We're pretty tribal in Wales, we're a country made up of mostly villages, and that is reflected in how three of the four regions have struggled to engage the wider rugby public.

The Ospreys are the only proper region, as it was envisioned; they took it on board, and have had the most success.

The Dragons tried to become a region, albeit half-heartedly, but there was too much in-fighting from the start. The politics is still there now, 12 years later, and they are still trying to convince people.

It went from Newport being one of the best supported teams in the UK at the turn of the century, to crowds of three or four thousand turning up for the Dragons that first season. Although they've risen since then, they've got nowhere near the same level since. After some promising signs early on, the team has never reached the same heights either.

The Ebbw/Newport relationship went sour pretty quickly, I think down to too many strong personalities on the different sides.

I don't believe David Moffett (former WRU chief executive, from Australia, who oversaw the change to regional rugby in 2003) ever fully understood the Welsh psyche and the implications of the changes he was imposing.

As players, we just had to say, "Right, let's get on with it," and that's what we did. Mike Ruddock was heading it up, with Clive Griffiths as his assistant, with a side cobbled together from the players they managed to keep from the two clubs after we'd lost a lot from both squads, mainly the foreign players.

We gelled together well as a squad and the 'no one likes us, we don't care attitude' was fostered within the group.

We were the 'mongrel mob', yet we went into the last weekend of that first season with an outside chance of winning the whole league. Ultimately, we lost in Leinster and finished third, behind the Scarlets and Ulster, but it was a fantastic season for us given everything we'd been through.

Percy Montgomery was one of the foreigners we'd kept and he was inspirational that season while we had some great youngsters who made their mark.

As fate goes, the view was that Mike had done so well with us that he ended up replacing Steve Hansen as Wales head coach at the end of the season, and he took Clive with him. It was fantastic for them but it didn't help us at all.

Obviously, given my history with Steve, and how well I had done for the Dragons under Mike, I believed that I'd soon be back in the Wales squad. I'd played a lot of games under him that year and he knew exactly what I could do so I genuinely believed that would count for something.

Unfortunately, I'd say now that the ghosts of that row were maybe still hanging around the Vale.

A number of Steve's coaches were still involved and must have had a view on the incident that didn't reflect well on me, and I had to wait almost another year before I finally had the call off Mike.

After a year where, under Mike and Clive, we'd created something against all odds at the Dragons, one year in we were starting again almost.

Declan Kidney was appointed to replace Mike. A quality coach from Ireland, with a great reputation, he had coached the national Under 19 team back home before taking the main job with Munster and getting to two Heineken Cup finals. He was assistant coach of the Irish national team when he agreed to replace Mike and everybody thought it was a fantastic appointment, one that would allow the Dragons to really kick on.

We all met with Declan, we were on board, but within weeks he had changed his mind and left to take the Leinster job! Clearly, he took one look at us and did a complete U-turn. We were back to square one.

Pre-season was well underway by the time we found out who was going to be the new coach and to say it was something of a shock appointment really would be a huge understatement.

We ended up appointing a rugby league coach from Australia called Chris Anderson.

Now, Chris had a great reputation in league, coaching teams to titles in both Australia and England, as well as winning the World Cup with his home country. That's a pretty impressive CV by anyone's standards.

It was just he'd never coached in union, ever! I got on well with him but there's no hiding place when you are stood in front of the group in team meetings and talking about the 13, and not 15. We'd lost two men to the sin bin before we'd started!

His character, and what he stood for, was really good. The problem he had, whether it was real or imagined, was that because he had no union background, it was easy for anyone not selected, or who was pissed off with something he did, to point the finger.

When that happens, rightly or wrongly, the environment starts creaking a little bit and unfortunately, that was what happened during Chris' year in charge,

His principles around the game were sound, even if he didn't have the technical understanding, but I think certain senior players, pushed by certain coaches who were pulling the strings maybe, made life difficult for him at times.

It was quite a brutal year, to be honest. There was a lot of undermining going on, with information being fed to the press, to 'Mr Gwent', Robin Davey, in particular.

Chris had his failures as a coach, coming from the background he did, don't get me wrong, but I felt that the knives were out for him from pretty early on and he was let down. He was hung out to dry.

It was actually a pretty good year on the field. The season started pretty well, we had some big wins in the early weeks, but as the environment changed, it fell away quite badly in the latter part of the season and there were some heavy defeats.

Saying that, we still managed to finish fourth, despite everything, and we were the second highest Welsh team again, with only the Ospreys above us as they won the league for the first time.

In the ten years since, the Dragons have never finished that high in the table again, so who knows what could have happened there if he had been given the right support?

I got on very well with Chris and I was sad at the way it played out. He really put his heart into it and deserved more.

With hindsight, he needed another coach alongside him who he trusted, one that was technically minded.

He couldn't trust anyone as he knew he was being stitched up, he knew there was whispering in corridors, and he couldn't turn to anyone within the environment.

My own form had been pretty good and in the spring of 2005 I finally received the call I'd been awaiting off Mike, taking me back into the Wales set-up, which was a phenomenal feeling.

We had a couple of chats in camp and it was obvious that my concerns had been right, that my comments to the press a couple of years earlier had left a less than favourable impression on some of the coaches who were still involved.

I was back in the squad, but I wasn't really involved as Wales secured a first Grand Slam in 27 years.

I'd been the only player released back to their club ahead of the first weekend of the competition and that sort of gave me a marker that I hadn't really been forgiven. As far as I was concerned, the coaches had sent a clear signal that they didn't see me as likely to play.

Instead of preparing to play England at the Millennium Stadium, I headed to Dubai on an all expenses paid trip with the Dragons to play the Stormers from South Africa.

Now they were taking it very seriously, using it as pre-season prep ahead of the new Super Rugby season, but for us it was a jolly, and a very good one at that. They were drinking Coke at all the functions around the game, we had a Jack Daniels in ours!

We'd gone out there missing seven first-choice players on international duty and it was a social trip for us with a game of rugby in the middle as an inconvenience. We wanted to enjoy the best that Dubai had to offer.

We actually made quite a good fist of it in the game itself and led 17–7 after half an hour before the differing pre-game preparations came to the fore and they scored 40 unanswered points!

The following afternoon we watched Wales beating

England, sitting around the pool on beanbags, supping a concoction called Bullfrog that took quite a bit of drinking if I'm honest, with a huge projector beaming the game out, and had a pretty good day of it.

We got back to Wales on the Monday, a bit weary after a good week. I reported to the Vale on the Tuesday, to be told that I'd been selected on the bench against Italy that Saturday because Ryan Jones had injured his shoulder in the England game. The news certainly helped me shake the hangover pretty quickly!

I hadn't been involved since 2003 so things had moved on, there were different moves, different calls, so it really was a tough week of getting up to scratch as quick as I could.

The game in Rome was to be my only involvement in a historic campaign as I carried the weight of my comments to the press around the Vale with me.

While I was disappointed with my lack of game time, and I genuinely feel a bit of a fraud when people list 'Grand Slam winner – 2005' among my achievements, it really was a great tournament and, probably, the best of all the modern Grand Slams because we'd waited so long for one.

The style of rugby was excellent, there was some brilliant interplay for some great tries, and it was a real crest of the wave.

The game against Ireland to win it was superb, they really played some amazing stuff and the team were worthy winners of a wonderful championship success.

When I talk about that Grand Slam now though, I call it my cameo Grand Slam, like a well-known actor who has a bit part, walks into one scene and says his lines before exiting stage right.

My focus as a successful Six Nations drew to a close was the summer tour to North America. It was a Lions year, with a tour to New Zealand that summer under Clive Woodward.

Even with an Englishman as coach, as Grand Slam winners we were certain to have a sizable representation with the Lions, so I viewed it as my chance to really re-establish myself in the Welsh set-up while they were away.

There was one game in Connecticut against the USA and then a match in Toronto, against Canada. Given my time in Canada a few years earlier, playing for the Nomads, I was particularly looking forward to that one and catching up with a few old friends.

Again, as with my Grand Slam experience, it turned out to be quite a disappointment.

I came off the bench in a win over the USA on the first weekend, it was a good team performance and we won 77–3.

I thought then that I'd have a good shout to start in Toronto the following weekend, particularly after Ryan Jones was parachuted into the Lions tour and flown down to New Zealand a day or two ahead of our game against Canada.

Instead, Luke Charteris and Rob Sidoli started with Brent on the bench, which stung a little bit. Brent had been first choice for a couple of years now and was well established, so they knew exactly what he could do and what he gave the team.

I was trying to punch my way back in, and this was kind of a 'home game' for me in a Test match which was as much of a foregone conclusion as you were ever going to get, if we're honest.

This isn't a personal thing against Brent at this point. I have to stress this as I do understand how it could come across.

I always had an awful lot of respect for him as a player and loved going up against him. I just didn't see any point in playing the tried and tested in these games, and still don't. I believed that they should have been looking at the wider group. I felt that if they weren't going to play people on the fringes in these games, when would they give us chance to show what we could do?

So, my 'homecoming' to Toronto proved to be a damp squib and, once again, I was left to focus on domestic rugby and another change of coach.

CHAPTER 5

A stroke of luck

GOING INTO THE new season I wanted to put my international frustrations behind me and focus on helping the Dragons build on what had been two good years.

With Chris Anderson leaving at the end of his one-year contract, change was inevitable, another season at Rodney Parade and another coach.

This time it was a return for an old Newport favourite, Paul 'Tommy' Turner.

As a player, he had been a skilful outside half and a reliable goal kicker, and still held the Newport points record, so he didn't have to win people over in the same way that Chris had failed to. People were going to be behind him from the start.

As a coach, he'd been at some big clubs and built up a decent record, both as a backs coach and as the main man, working with clubs like Sale, Saracens and Gloucester.

He came to the Dragons after three years at Harlequins, unfortunately after they had been relegated from the top division in England for the first time.

Leigh Jones, who had been Newport head coach previously and was forwards coach at the Dragons under Chris Anderson, was to be his assistant.

There had been a lot of turmoil around the place two years earlier, Ruddock taking over amidst all the political wrangling off the field, but I take my hat off to Mike and Clive.

With Mike's managerial skills and Clive's coaching and enthusiasm, they ran a good ship that year and turned what should have been a very average team into a pretty good one.

Don't get me wrong, we still had good players there, the likes of Michael Owen, Ceri Sweeney, Andy Marinos, but there wasn't any real depth. Most people looking in from the outside thought that we were going to struggle, we weren't up to it, but plenty of people took their chance with both hands.

I've been involved in teams that can only be described as star-studded, but the collective didn't work as a team, for whatever reason. Under Mike at the Dragons, and for most of the season under Chris, that wasn't the case. We were written off, there was no way we were expected to win some of the games that we did, but we were a team that gave everything and the credit for that goes to the coaches.

I think that raised expectations. The Dragons had twice finished inside the top four, but it was unrealistic to think that we could continue defying those expectations when we still had the weakest squad of the four regions. The constant turnover of coaches, with changes of outlook, also didn't help.

Tommy was a really good coach but, if I'm honest, where he struggled, particularly towards the end of my time there, was in his man management ability.

Top-end man managers know exactly what they have to do to get the best out of the boys. I suppose it's no different in business; the most successful companies manage their employees really well, they look after them.

Mike did that, and whatever the downfalls of Chris' time in the hot seat, you could see that he had that ability as well, but I think at times Tommy struggled with that.

He always had the trump card in his back pocket that we didn't have the facilities at the Dragons, we didn't have the same funding as everyone else. I think it was too easy to say, "How can we perform, we train on a cabbage patch?"

Don't get me wrong, it was true, we did have terrible facilities, but I don't think that's what players want, or need, to hear day in, day out.

It gives them an excuse for not performing and it makes it easier to accept failure in the group if everyone thinks that way. It's very easy to quickly talk yourself into a vicious cycle of underachieving and failure, and I think that's what happened at the Dragons.

I knew that I was coming towards the end of my contract at the end of the 2006/07 season.

A year or so before that, I was starting to assess my personal situation.

I was fast approaching my 30th birthday at that point and, by now, was a regular member of the Wales squad, starting in most games as I put the legacy of my spat with Steve Hansen behind me.

After my frustrations around the 2005 Grand Slam and the summer tour, I was selected for the November internationals but found myself in the usual position as chief tackle bag holder and cheerleader as we lost heavily to New Zealand and really struggled against Fiji, winning 11–10.

I was gutted, I really was, as I just felt it was Groundhog Day for me and we were back in Toronto.

Having been overlooked for the New Zealand game, the Fiji match was the one in the series that we were expected to win with ease and, for that reason, would be the one fixture of the autumn where the coaches could traditionally experiment.

Key players would be rested to ensure they were available for the tougher games ahead. It was the one game I felt they were bound to pick me, to protect Brent.

They picked Brent, alongside Charts.

I remember saying to Michael Owen, "If they won't pick me against Fiji, of the four games in this series, then I'll never get picked. What's the point in me being here?"

He was a few years younger than me, but he was always something of an old head on young shoulders. His advice this time was, "You can't get too despondent about things, your fortunes can change in a second. You just have to work hard and be ready when your opportunity comes."

I was still very much head in my hands at that point, the black rain cloud was over me, following me wherever I went.

I could see the curtain coming down on my international career.

However, as is the way of pro sport, someone's injury pain is always someone else's relief, just as had been the case back in 1999 when Gareth Llewellyn came in at my expense and ended up going to the World Cup.

Brent snapped his hamstring off the bone in the Fiji game and that was his season over. Mike came up to me afterwards to reiterate what he'd said in our chat a few days earlier, about fortunes changing and having to take your opportunity when it arose, and he was right.

It was a very bad injury and while, as a human being, I sympathised with him, as a professional rugby player and a rival for the same shirt, my only thought was, "Well, they've got to pick me for South Africa next week now, surely?"

What I've learned over the years is that you can be almost down and out, up against the ropes, then there's a little twist of fate and you spring from third or fourth choice right back up the pecking order. That is what happened to me that November.

Going into the next game, against South Africa, we set up in training at the start of the week with Luke and Rob starting and me on the bench, but it was clear that Luke had ankle issues.

He could hardly walk, so I knew I was in with a sniff. I trained all week as if I was starting, in my head that was what was happening, even though when it came to naming the team he was included.

Charts is a great guy, he was my teammate at the Dragons, and he said to me after the team was publicly announced, "There's no chance I'm playing, there's no way I'll be able to do it."

That's how it worked out. I finally had the nod instead of him. I had a decent enough game despite the loss; I played in the win over Australia the following weekend and never looked back. I went on a run of games in the team that went right through to the next World Cup two years later.

I'd gone from one of the lowest points of my career and, just like that, everything turned around for me.

It's the way of professional sport that you need a spot of fortune, usually around somebody else's misfortune, to give you that chance. Nobody wishes anyone to get injured, far from it, but everybody knows, at the back of their head, that if you aren't being selected, as I wasn't, that something has to change.

That something is usually injury or someone's bad form. The key is that when that chance arrives, you have to be ready to take it. If you aren't prepared for it, the next man in the queue will take it instead.

Off the back of the win over Australia, we went into the 2006 Six Nations on a bit of a high. After so many years of struggles we were defending champions and, accordingly, expectations among the Welsh public were soaring.

However, as is often the way, scratch beneath the surface and the picture can be very different. It's fair to say that at that point I was probably still something of an outsider in the squad, someone who had been brought into the camp after so long out of favour and, despite the on-field success, I had been sensing some slight disharmony in the camp, all the way back to the previous Six Nations.

Steve Hansen had gone, and a lot of players had got on really well with him.

I sensed that in certain sections there was a disgruntled feeling that Mike was taking the credit for the work that had been done before he'd taken charge the previous year, and also, for the work still being done every day by people who had been involved with the previous regime.

In fairness to Mike, he was the head guy and was fronting everything. He was very good with the press, and while he would coach, he was excellent at managing and organising. He had trust in his coaches to take responsibility for certain areas and would allow them to go out and do their job.

As the 2006 Six Nations got underway we started with a

heavy defeat at Twickenham, a result guaranteed to bring everyone back down to earth.

The next week we laboured to a 28–18 win in Cardiff over Scotland, who had played for an hour a man short after Scott Murray was red-carded for kicking me in the face, opening me up.

It was retaliation for a late tackle by myself that resulted in me getting a yellow, despite my protests that it couldn't have been late, I'd got there as quick as I could!

I think it was Jonathan Davies who said in commentary that they needed a calendar to time the tackle, not a stopwatch!

It was a terrible game really but the extra man allowed us to take the initiative away from them as time went on and get our campaign going after the disappointment at Twickenham.

Post-match we had the usual media duties and function and everything seemed to be business as normal. There was seemingly nothing untoward in the air and with the win behind us we had something to build on ahead of our next game, away to Italy in two weeks.

That was on the Sunday and the following day some of the boys had press at the Vale. As the media hoards were turning up there was a real swirl of activity, there were rumours flying around that something was afoot and that there was going to be a big announcement.

I genuinely hadn't seen it coming, but by Tuesday, Valentine's Day, we were all aware that Mike had resigned and it was being announced that night.

I had the same sort of, 'Here we go again, another Welsh rugby crisis,' feeling that I'd felt in South Africa and during Grannygate. I seemed to be at the heart of the low times, having missed the ten-game winning run under Henry and only played my cameo part in the Grand Slam.

We knew the press would be going for it and we'd have to keep our heads down as there would be rockets going off above us.

It's no secret that I hadn't seen eye to eye with Hansen, as I've already documented but, as the outsider from that period in the squad, I could sense there was still a very close attachment to him within elements of the group.

They'd been on a bit of a journey with him. The World Cup that I'd missed in 2003 had become a real turning point in quite a few careers. The whole set-up had taken quite a hammering from press and supporters alike in the year leading up to the competition, with his mantra of performance over results not really striking the right chord with the public, given a poor run of results.

Nobody had given them any kind of chance in the tournament, and the opening games against Canada and Italy, while wins, hadn't really seen them catch fire.

However, they were followed by two memorable games against New Zealand and England which, although both ending in defeat, had seemingly restored faith and pride, inside and outside of the camp.

Going into that New Zealand game, it seemed to everyone on the outside that he got lucky. I, and just about everybody else who watched on ITV Wales that Sunday morning, may be wrong, but it looked as though he rested a lot of people for the New Zealand game, conceding defeat and saving them for England, and the boys who came in did superbly well and almost beat the All Blacks.

On that occasion he was right, it was about performance and not result, as you could see the confidence that the team got from going so close and they all grew off the back of it.

They'd been struggling and one backs-to-the-wall performance seemed to see everything click. I genuinely don't think Steve Hansen expected those boys to play that well but he certainly owed them one as I think they saved his job and, ultimately, extended my international exodus.

Cheers, boys!

It had been a tough time for everybody involved but, after they came through those World Cup games together, I think there was a bond within the group and a lot of people got close to Steve and Johnno.

With hindsight, that was a hard thing for Mike to deal with coming into the job in 2004. He brought Clive Griffiths into the set-up with him but the rest of the support team was pretty much unchanged.

Mike would do his bit, around the scrum and whatever, but as I've already said, a lot of his work was being done away from the training pitch. He was the captain of the ship, so to speak, managing and organising, delegating work to those who he felt had the right capabilities.

I think he would have been better off if he had come in with a clean sweep and brought all his own staff with him. That's not to be critical of anyone involved at the time, but it stands to reason that if he wanted to be his own man then he needed his own men.

Although Hansen had gone, the players who had worked with him and his team still had a relationship with the staff who had stayed on, which in reality was the vast majority of the coaching, technical and support staff. His legacy ran right through the national set-up, he was everywhere in spirit, even if he had long since departed.

There's a psychological phenomenon called Stockholm syndrome, where hostages begin to empathise and sympathise with their captors over a period of time, even to the point of defending and identifying with their captors.

For the boys under Steve who had spent months locked in the Vale Hotel – so much so it became known as the Jail of Glamorgan – there looks to be an element of that syndrome in how they grew to resent Mike.

It was a strange one for me. Because I wasn't involved throughout most of the Hansen era I didn't have that affinity that other people did. In fact, I actually knew Mike from the Dragons after I'd fallen out with Steve so, although I'd say I was neutral, I could understand if people disagreed with me about that.

I still had respect for Steve though, absolutely I did. I realised that the way I handled the whole situation of being left out of the World Cup squad hadn't been the right way to do so, and I had respect for the job he did and what the other players said about him.

The allegiances were too strong for Mike to overcome though, and I think that when he was awarded the OBE after the Grand Slam and headed off to Buckingham Palace, that resentment grew. Mike was heading up the team and that's the nature of team sport; when things go well the coach gets the plaudits and when things go wrong they are the ones who get sacked, not the players.

Less than 18 months later, I experienced one of the most poignant and upsetting things of my career, watching Gareth Jenkins making the lonely walk away from the Vale Hotel after getting sacked following the 2007 World Cup. Yet the players who had been involved in that failure, and I include myself in this, got away almost without a blemish on our reputation.

I think there was a fair degree of naivety about how people thought around the whole Ruddock situation.

Hansen had been very hands-on whereas Mike admittedly wasn't that hands-on, but he saw his role as facilitating others a lot more, trusting people and allowing them to be the expert in their particular field.

However, I believe that approach was misinterpreted in some quarters and used as something to challenge him over.

Once you got to the position where he was being questioned and challenged, I don't think there was anywhere for him to go really. He sensed that and decided it was time to come to a compromise.

Obviously there were a lot of caveats around his departure but it was done in a dignified way, allowing him to walk away. However, because of the caveats, because of the secrecy around the situation, it invited more questions than it answered, which helped nobody in the long run.

A lot has been written since then about player power forcing him out. I wouldn't agree with that despite what I've said; there was never a movement to get rid of him. I don't see that there were covert meetings to put him under pressure.

What I do believe is that there was resentment and he could see that for himself. All coaching jobs have a lifespan and he realised that it was time to get out.

If he'd had all his own coaches, his people in charge, and had done it his way from day one, then it would have been very different. He just couldn't beat the dynamics that were there from the start, and felt that it was time to move on.

The days after his resignation was announced – it was pretty crazy. The press had their line, the player power story. It wasn't quite like that, as I've tried to explain, and I understand that it may still not be clear to you reading this. The whole period was a pretty confused, murky and muddy time. Regardless, the vultures in the media were circling, ready to pick on the carcass of the Ruddock era.

We still had three games to go in the Six Nations. Scott Johnson took over as caretaker coach, and really, with such intense scrutiny on the group, we just had to keep our heads down once again, almost bury them in the sand.

It was a rough time for everybody involved with Wales through that period if I'm honest, whatever side of the fence you sat on.

The public loved Mike, he had a good public persona and, after all, had just delivered a first Grand Slam in 27 years. Memories were fresh of what had been a fantastic uplift in the Welsh national mood not a year earlier and the person they saw as responsible for that had, so they were reading in the paper, been forced out by the players.

People were being demonised, being vilified, and it really was a case of needing to get inside and close the doors on everybody else. We'll stick together. By saying nothing, Mike won the PR war.

Then we had the Alfie *Scrum V* thing a week later, which made everything more dramatic, more theatrical. It was a weird, weird time, and that was a suitably weird experience to put the icing on it.

For those unfamiliar with it, and surely there can't be a Welsh rugby fan from around that time who is honestly unfamiliar, Alfie, or Gareth Thomas, was our captain at the time and he agreed to appear on BBC Wales' flagship rugby programme the following weekend in order to directly answer questions of player power.

He had said, "I'm going on to defend you, boys."

It was quite bonkers television.

Alfie always was a player's player. He was a good guy and a good captain, but I would say that to a man, the squad were sat on their sofas thinking to themselves, 'Noooo, this is descending into disaster now.'

Also on the programme were Eddie Butler and Jonathan Davies, two former Wales players turned pundits. Eddie is a very clever bloke, a Cambridge Blue, and well connected. He prodded and prodded, like a child tormenting an insect with a stick, until Alfie eventually reacted, losing his cool, and you could see both Eddie and Jonathan pull back, thinking, 'I didn't expect that.'

Such was the trauma that Alfie then collapsed at home afterwards when watching it back, ending up hospitalised and missing the rest of the season.

It wasn't just car crash television, the entire situation had become a complete farce.

To be honest, after that circus, we were glad to be able to get our minds back on the rugby the following weekend.

With Johnno in temporary charge, we made little impression in the remaining three games though, as the player power row rumbled on in the background.

Johnno also ended up in the firing line in some quarters, albeit unfairly, as some of Mike's supporters in the press felt that he had maybe manipulated the players to get the outcome he wanted.

Like I've said, it wasn't a good time for anyone and it came as little surprise to anyone that we failed to win any of those three games before Johnno departed at the end of the Six Nations to take up a post with the Australian team.

In doing so he brought the curtain down on a forgettable few months for Wales. Our paths would cross again in the not too distant future but for now, at least, another colourful character took the spotlight in Welsh rugby.

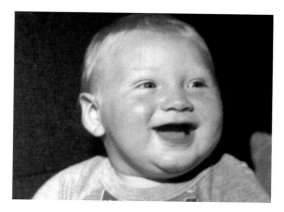

Quite the chunky baby here; if I'd kept that shape I'd have been straight in the front row.

An early family pic before my parents' divorce.

Getting some early nutrition into myself, the poor haircut theme has still stayed with me.

Receiving my Newport Youth player of the year trophy from my Grancha Bernard Gough who had played for Newport in the 1930s.

The caption says it all, Grancha in a Newport shirt.

NEWPORT ATHLETIC CLUB
FIRST XV.
SEASON 1938-39

Played 43.   Won 24.   Drawn 1.   Lost 18.   Points For: 403.   Points Against: 312.

V. M. GRIFFITHS   J. S. NIXON   W. G. JONES   J. C ADAMS   E. COLEMAN   J. C. JERMAN   W. H. TRAVERS   A. D. PRICE   A. J. BALE
(Football Hon. Sec.)   C. MOGFORD
                                                                                                                                        (Attendant)

L. T. EVANS   R. F. ALLEN   V. J. LAW   H. UZZELL   J. HAWKINS   W. G. LEGGE   J. T. KNOWLES
                              (Captain)   (Chairman)   (Vice-Captain)

B. GOUGH   D. LITTLE   K. LANCEY   W. H. M. BAKER

A young Goughy with my cousins, my haircuts still haven't gotten much better.

Larking around with my sister Michelle and niece Evie down in Llangennith.

With my Uncle Mike 'Mad Dog' Gough, the ironman likened in looks to Robert Redford, with the voice of Lionel Richie, and a massive character in the Gough family. We had organised this get-together as he was suffering badly with emphysema and that fateful night is when I faced the allegations that unfortunately he didn't live long enough to see overturned in the Appeal Courts.

Father and son.

An early action shot of me in Toronto Nomads colours. I enjoyed a great season in Canada, learning the ropes of senior rugby. I still have some great friends there 20 years later.

An early Newport RFC team photo.

A very skinny Goughy in the late 90s. I had to be, to keep up with Chris 'the one-man riot' Wyatt.

Young and fresh-faced in 2000. Fifteen years later and I'm a battered old man.

The reason I joined the Ospreys. A great bunch of lads and a winning culture. Leinster had the party already booked and we pulled the rug from under them. Good times indeed.

This has to go in as, when I get fat and middle aged, this will be a reminder that I was once fit. Shameless.

I've just completed my first solo flight in Toronto after staying on there after the Welsh Tour in 2005.

Finally gaining my Private Pilot's Licence in Cardiff in 2007. Pictured with chief flying instructor, Chris Good.

Am I looking chunky here or is it just because I'm sandwiched between two racing snakes? Jammo and Boycey (Dafydd James and Mark Jones) are two great finishers and proper characters in their own right.

A very young Alun Wyn Jones at the 2007 World Cup cap presentation evening. A full head of hair and looking lush, as he would say. Probably the best second row I've played with.

A Rugby World Cup warm-up game in 2007 versus Argentina. This is the match where I first noticed the problem with my heart, although it would take several years to diagnose.

One thing I've learned is never to shout this man's nickname across a crowded airport (BOMB). An absolute legend of the game and, in my opinion, he was treated poorly at the end of his Wales career.

Maybe, in hindsight, a hospitality day at the races in Paris, a week before our final group game against Fiji in Nantes, wasn't the best bit of planning.

Bobby Bouché or 'The Waterboy' as Duncan Jones would call me. Billy Whizz did have sharp feet. Some you hit, some you miss. Ryan is just giving him a pat on the back in this shot, saying well done.

With Newport RFC legend David 'Muddy' Waters. My first game for Newport in 1996 was number 703 (and the last) for him. An amazing career that towers over my 400 plus games.

From a Newport RFC legend to a worldwide legend, Gary Teichmann. It was a real privilege to play in the same pack as this guy.

In the mix of formation school out of North Weald, Essex. I'm pictured in the yellow and blue plane in front. The dangers became real as the next day we lost two people in a fatal crash whilst tail chasing.

Flying instructor and RAF Hercules pilot, Si Hulme, who sadly lost his life in that incident. Our flight back to Swansea was very solemn.

OK, who's put the ground the wrong way up? Clowning about over south Wales.

I flew myself and a friend, Martin Zwart, to Dublin for the Ospreys second Rabo PRO12 play-off victory over Leinster. Here we are passing by the Aviva Stadium.

Just tipped in for the 'Run and Break' at Swansea Airport. I've got the air conditioning on full.

Going to bed early at a military base after a fundraising game has consequences. My first encounter with Mark 'Dott' Perkins, which led to a great friendship, with me eventually being best man at his wedding. This event got me involved with the Hire a Hero charity of which I'm now a patron.

It's not just clingfilm pranks when Dott is around. A young Alun Wyn Jones falling foul to the banter after crashing out early after a Test match in Paris. Dott almost got walloped when Alun Wyn woke up next to this strange naked ginger bloke.

Dott is now a physio to the stars, which means I get to blag my way to events in support. Davina McCall is one of the many celebrities he now works with.

Stag do at the Munich beer festival. Well, I'm a lady of course, in true *Little Britain* style.

A fundraising dinner at Birmingham City FC ahead of my first Hire a Hero expedition.

Taking a new angle at the ice bucket challenge. This would have remained private but someone decided to put the clip on YouTube, so what the hell!

Doing my bit to clean the three inches of dead flies off the windscreen.

This might look easy but, in rigid summit boots and being over 18 stone, this river crossing was sketchy to say the least!

Hire a Hero Mount Elbrus climb. Carrying the heavy kit up and down from lower base camp to high base camp didn't do the back any good.

Acclimatisation day, past 4,000 metres, finished a few of the gang off. I suffered a burnt hooter.

Unfortunately this was as high as we got. The weather closed in and a few tough decisions had to be made.

CHAPTER 6

All Blacks and cheats

GARETH JENKINS TOOK over the reins from Johnno in the spring of 2006. A Llanelli legend, he had spent his whole career, player and coach, at Stradey Park in west Wales.

He played almost 300 times for the Scarlets, including their famous win over the All Blacks in 1972, and went on to coach them for more than 20 years, winning league titles and cups, and twice taking them to the semi-final of the Heineken Cup.

He had also been assistant coach with Wales when they won the Five Nations in 1994 and went with Clive Woodward on the Lions tour in 2005.

By anyone's standards that's a pretty impressive CV, certainly as good as anyone in Wales at the time.

The Welsh media had certainly been beating his drum, declaring him the people's choice, particularly after he had very publicly lost out on the job to Mike Ruddock a few years earlier.

He is a brilliant bloke to be fair, I don't think you'll find anyone who has a bad word about him as a person.

He just has one of those likeable personalities that means he can get away with anything. People just gravitate to him.

There's a story about a function he was at, with Sir Alex Ferguson in attendance as speaker. Gareth just jumped into the seat next to him and within minutes Sir Alex was roaring with laughter at this crazy bloke from Llanelli.

One of his big strengths is his motivational speaking; he is capable of getting the hairs on the back of your neck standing on end. But he can go from one extreme to the other in seconds.

He can have you feeling incredibly emotional and destroy it all within seconds by virtue of just being Gareth! I remember sitting in the Vale when he gave a real fire and brimstone speech; it was a tremendous speech and when you looked around the room you could see the throats going, the Adam's apples bobbing in several throats.

As he is just getting to what is clearly going to be his high point, he takes his jacket off, puts it over a chair and, as he stands in front of us, he's got the most ridiculous Simon Cowell going on, with his waistband almost up around his nipples. Talk about spoiling the moment. Everyone was head down, not daring to catch a colleague's eye, shoulders shaking as we tried to keep the laughter in.

There was another game against Argentina, where he came in at half-time and warned us that, "Boys, you've got to be up for this, it's going to be a real battle of nutrition." I presume he meant attrition!

He was a master at mangling words, a famous one was physitensity, again, presumably a cross of physicality and intensity!

He'd clearly learnt from Mike's mistakes as he was able to negotiate his own coaching team, bringing with him Nigel Davies and Robin McBryde (who he'd worked with at the Scarlets), Rowland Phillips (who'd coached at Neath and the Ospreys), and my old Ponty and Wales teammate Neil Jenkins.

First up for the new coach was a tour of Argentina, two Tests, the first of which was in Patagonia.

For those of you who don't know, Patagonia is home to a historic Welsh settlement where even today the native Welsh language survives and more than 50,000 locals are of Welsh descent.

It was a fantastic tour to be a part of because of the history and the culture.

All the Welsh-speaking players headed off to Trelew, one of the original settlements, to meet some of the locals, including a lady in her nineties, a Welsh speaker whose parents had moved to Patagonia when she was a child.

As they were chatting to her she basically pointed at Nathan Brew and asked in Welsh, "What's he doing here?" Now Brewy heard this so answered, "I'm here as part of the Welsh squad, I'm a Welsh speaker and I wanted to come along and see this place." To which the lady let off a big, high-pitched noise, almost a shriek, and said at the top of her voice in shock, "Negro." Brewy just sighed and shrugged his shoulders as everyone else absolutely wet themselves with laughter.

That's the cultural divide for you, she was 90-odd years old and had been there since she was six, and had never seen a Welsh-speaking black person.

It was quite a relaxed tour. I wouldn't go so far as to say there was a drinking culture but there was a good social scene. It wasn't as intense an environment as previous Welsh camps I'd been a part of.

We lost the first Test, a cracking match, 27–25, in a settlement called Puerto Madryn, an absolutely stunning place with huge Welsh heritage. There were four Welsh debuts that day, all from the Ospreys – Alun Wyn Jones, Ian Evans, James Hook and Richard Hibbard. Not a bad crop of youngsters, who would go on to serve Wales with real distinction through a very successful period.

We then lost 45–27 in Buenos Aires where we were outplayed unfortunately, but in the spirit of the tour, the defeat didn't let it spoil the night as the post-match function disintegrated into something that can only be described as like something from the Wild West.

The trouble was that Ian Evans was having to face a citing commissioner at the same time and same place as the function and I recall Alan 'Thumper' Phillips, the team manager, having to come out of the citing meeting to try and calm everyone down as the bread rolls were flying around the room.

Later that year, in November, I played my one and only Test match against New Zealand.

As is always the case in these fixtures, we lost. It wasn't even one of those occasional years where we pushed them close as they outscored us five tries to one, Sitiveni Sivivatu scoring three. It finished 45–10.

However, personally, that game is more memorable for the reaction to some of my pre-match comments to the media.

I was sat at the press conference a few days before the game, feeling pretty confident as I dealt with some easy questions. It was at this point I was asked for my opinion on New Zealand cheating at the breakdown.

I remembered one of my first coaches at Newport, Steve 'Junna' Jones, who actually died a year later, who had quipped that they were cheats but they were honest cheats and they got away with it. It's all about boundaries and pushing them as far as you can. If you don't get pulled up for it then it's fair game.

At the time I thought that I could be clever about it, that it was a fun thing to say to the press, so I reiterated those words. They were honest cheats and they got away with it. That's what everyone is trying to do.

In my own mind it was quite well said, it was quite funny and everyone would see it like that and take it for what it was.

It turned out that that wasn't the case.

I think the headline in the *Western Mail* was 'Gough brands New Zealand cheaters'.

The last thing I'd wanted to do was wind them up.

I'd left the press conference without a care in the world, was sat down in the Vale having a cup of coffee, when Martyn Williams came out saying, "Goughy, what the hell have you said in there?"

I was all nervous, "What do you mean?"

"You've just called New Zealand cheats. They're asking everybody what do they think about Goughy's comments, he's called them cheats."

"No, no, don't worry about it, it was tongue in cheek."

I could see the look on his face and it dawned on me that he was serious and there could be repercussions.

By now the nerves were starting to twitch and there was a realisation of, 'Oh, no, have I made a bit of an arse of myself?'

I spoke to Thumper about it, explained what had happened and how it was meant, talking about what Junna used to say.

Thumper got straight on the phone to Steve Hansen, who by now was assistant coach to Graham Henry with New Zealand.

At his press conference the following day, Steve was duly asked by one of the *Western Mail* writers for his views on my comments. Now, we had history in terms of me saying the wrong thing to the press, so he didn't have to do it. He certainly didn't owe me anything but, all credit to him, he didn't just shoot the argument dead, he went further than that, taking the opportunity to highlight how the press had stitched me up.

It was very much a case of, 'Thanks Steve, and lesson learned,' on my behalf. I had just turned 30, and was very much a senior player by now, but it was an eye-opener for me about how they can lead you down the path they want to take you without you even realising, to give them the story they want.

Back at the Dragons, things had started to decline on and off the field quite clearly, and I made a conscious decision that I wanted to make a career move.

I had a few offers on the table, but it was the Ospreys that really attracted me.

When I'd been in the Wales camp I'd spoken at great length to people like Duncan Jones, Sonny Parker, Ryan Jones and Jonathan Thomas, and I liked what they had to say about the ambition they had at the Ospreys.

What I saw was similar to Pontypridd when I'd gone there a few years earlier, a good tight unit, working-class boys, a well-run club with real ambition, and I wanted to be a part of something like that.

Like I said, I was 30 by now and, I had to ask myself, would I get another opportunity like that one?

The way I could see things sliding at the Dragons, it was clear that I was at a career crossroads and, if I wanted to win things, I had to get out of my comfort zone, get into a different environment and see if I would sink or swim.

That year (2007), the Ospreys won a second league title in three seasons while the Dragons finished ninth in the league, down one on the previous season and a world away from the excitement of the first two years of regional rugby.

At least this time we managed to defeat Italian side Calvisano in a play-off match to qualify for the Heineken Cup in what was my final game in a Dragons shirt, for now at least.

The previous year we had failed to achieve even that heady height, suffering what was a pretty humiliating home defeat to Parma in a similar play-off.

There didn't seem to be any kind of strategy in place there. If money was being invested then it was being invested badly. Everything seemed ad hoc. We went from being a really competitive side to one that lacked any consistency or direction. You're a product of your environment and I don't think that the environment there at the time was conducive to us pushing on to be successful.

By contrast, the ambition at the Ospreys was huge. I remember being in Wales camp for the Six Nations that spring and Mike Phillips, who was at the Blues at the time, giving me the nudge-nudge, wink-wink treatment, asking me about signing for the Ospreys. I didn't say anything, but it became clear pretty soon why he'd been like that when it was announced he was signing for the Ospreys as well.

In fact that same summer, as well as Mike and myself, they also announced the signing of British Lion, Mark Taylor, and All Black, Marty Holah, confirming that I had made the right move if it was ambition I wanted.

A rugby player has a pretty short shelf life and at the time

I moved from the Dragons I had to ask myself – if I stayed there, could I see myself influencing things and helping to improve the place?

The genuine answer to that, given the environment at the time, was no. So the next question was – did I want to test myself in a far more demanding environment, or was I prepared to take the easy option?

People have said to me that the decision to go there was a money one, that I was joining a region that was just buying up all the galacticos. I can honestly say without fear of any contradiction from anyone that I was offered more money to stay at the Dragons at that time.

I took less money to play for the Ospreys, as the motivator for me making that move was a desire for success. I wanted to win things, I wanted to be involved in big games and I wanted to play for a team that shared that ambition.

Before I would actually pull on an Ospreys jersey, there was the small matter of a World Cup on the horizon later that year and, having failed to make it to the 1999 and 2003 tournaments, I was determined not to miss out for a third time.

Although I was firmly established in the squad at this stage, I refused to take anything for granted given what had happened to me previously.

First up was a tour to Australia in May, four months before the competition got underway. However, it was quite a strange set-up as Gareth opted to split his extended squad into two, with 28 people going Down Under for two difficult Tests, and 18, including myself, staying in Wales for a training camp.

That decision divided opinion in the press, and with the 'stay at home' 18 being perhaps the core of the Six Nations squad a couple of months earlier, the travelling party were unfairly labeled as no-hopers as they headed south.

Watching that first Test at home, it was unbelievable really. We led 17–0 early on and although they came back into it, we were still ahead with time-up.

Unfortunately for us, Gareth Cooper failed to find touch with a kick that would have meant game over, and they then kept the ball alive, going through eight or nine phases to score and win the game.

Off the back of that one, the second Test was far more clear-cut as we lost 31–0.

A few days after that game, just after the boys had returned, I was on my computer when Ceri Sweeney popped up on my Instant Messenger. I asked was he going on holiday now he was back, and his reply was along the lines of, "Holiday, I've just been on holiday!"

It seemed that the relaxed environment from Argentina a year earlier had been replicated.

There is a now legendary, almost mythical, and often repeated quote from the tour, relating to their first night in Australia, where the boys were on the bus from the airport and Gareth took the microphone at the front to explain that although he knew all the recommended procedures to deal with jetlag, he always found that the best way was to go out and have a few beers.

I'm told that they followed his advice to the letter. Just days later a widely written off Wales team should have beaten Australia out there for the first time in almost 40 years, so there must have been something in his methods!

Having stayed at home and missed the tour, I did eventually make it into a World Cup squad at the third attempt.

We went into the competition without any kind of form.

I was fortunate to miss an incredible 62–5 defeat against England at Twickenham, but I was back the following weekend to play in a disjointed win over Argentina in Cardiff, before a 25-point defeat at home to France in our final warm-up game.

Once the competition got underway in September, the first three games probably went with the form book.

We beat Canada in the opener, taking our time to crack them before our superior fitness allowed us to pull away in the second half to win 42–17. We then lost 32–20 to Australia. I'd started both games but was left out of a much-changed team for the easiest game of the pool stage that saw us record a big win over Japan.

Everything was now on the final match of the pool stage, against Fiji, in Nantes.

Both teams had recorded similar results, the same wins and losses, but we went into the game in second place by virtue of our superior points' record that was almost entirely down to the big win over Japan.

Every day throughout that competition we would be given an itinerary for the day. On the morning of the Fiji game we were given our itinerary for that day.

The thing was, that morning, a few hours ahead of this must-win game against Fiji, and knowing that defeat would mean we were going home, the itinerary we were given included post-match activity and, for the following day, our flight details to travel to Marseille for the quarter-final, along with a team preview for South Africa who were waiting in the old port city for the winners of this game.

I'll emphasise that this was already printed out and given to the players before we'd played the deciding fixture.

Undoubtedly, I would say that the coaches that weekend took their eye off the prize a bit there.

They were concentrating on playing South Africa the following week, looking further down the line, but fell at the hurdle that was right in front of them. Did that transmit to the players? It's hard to say, but what I do know is that we got dragged into the kind of game that Fiji love, we played to their strengths and ultimately paid the price.

It was probably an epic game to watch if you were a neutral but, coming off the bench as I did late on, it was awful to watch and even worse to be a part of.

We were 22 points behind at one point in the first half, trailing 25–3, but managed to turn that around to lead by four points going into the final quarter.

Fiji weren't finished and retook the lead, only for Martyn Williams to score a late interception try that we thought had won it.

Somehow we contrived to lose it from there, a TMO decision going Fiji's way with time just about up. Fiji had a first ever win against Wales, after nine attempts, and their first quarter-final in 20 years. Wales were going home the following day, regardless of what the itinerary in our kit bag told us.

Gareth immediately came under intense media pressure, with just six wins from 20 games and this first round exit from the World Cup.

In the dressing room after the game he had been very upbeat, insisting he wasn't going to walk away, or let us down.

He was a good man, someone who gave absolutely everything to the job. He had enjoyed real success previously and had experienced different environments.

The big job had proven too much for him though. In Wales the head coach of the national rugby team is a pretty unique job, with pressures that, I'd imagine, nothing could prepare you for. You are under constant scrutiny from a nation of bar room experts; everyone seemingly has an opinion and wants to make sure it is heard.

The following day, as we headed home to Wales instead of taking the flight to Marseille to play South Africa as per the schedule, was a very emotional one.

Roger Lewis, fairly recently appointed as chief executive of the WRU, acted swiftly and brutally, meeting with Gareth in the hotel on the morning after the game and before we left for home. He told him that he was fired.

Despite his bullishness post-match, I suspect Gareth had foreseen this coming. It didn't make it any easier on anyone, though.

Understandably, it was a pretty subdued journey given what had happened to Gareth, who remained a popular figure among the squad. As the bus was approaching the Vale, Gareth stood up at the front, dressed in his WRU suit and tie, to stop the bus. He told us, "Boys, if you don't mind I'll get off here," and with all the press waiting at the front of the hotel he walked alone around the back roads to the training barn, to avoid them and the inevitable questions.

It was one of those moments, looking out of the bus window as he walked away, carrier bag in his hand, where chins just dropped. There was absolute silence on the bus. He is such a proud guy, a proud Welshman and a proud rugby man.

It was such a sad moment and not the kind of end befitting a great servant of the game in Wales, regardless of an early World Cup exit. I believe that he deserved to be, and should have been, treated with far more dignity than he was at the time.

I can only imagine how much he was hurting at the pretty public humiliation he suffered, which seemed designed purely to generate the right newspaper headlines.

CHAPTER 7

Grand Slam glory

GIVEN WALES' EARLY exit from the 2007 Rugby World Cup, I reported for duty at the Ospreys a little earlier than I'd hoped for, when most people hadn't even turned their calendar over to the page marked October yet.

The set-up was like chalk and cheese in comparison to the Dragons and settling in was made so much easier because I knew so many of the boys from the Wales squad.

I'd lived with many of them for the previous three or four months so it was an easy transition, despite the obvious step up in intensity from where I'd been for the last seven years.

It was an exciting time for me personally. I'd always lived around Gwent and although Swansea was only 50 miles away and I could have commuted, I moved myself lock, stock and barrel, to immerse myself in the place. Just a month or so away from my 31st birthday I was finally cutting the umbilical cord that still existed when I lived close to my parents.

Swansea is a great city to live in, on the coast with some fantastic beaches and countryside, as well as plenty going on in town, so it was very easy to settle. In fact, this place is my home now, I can't ever see me leaving Swansea, whatever the future brings and wherever it takes me.

Lyn Jones was the head coach at the Ospreys, and had been since day one in 2003. A former Neath and Llanelli flanker who had played for Wales a handful of times in the Nineties, I had heard a lot about Lyn 'the lip', that he was something of a maverick, almost an eccentric genius, although I didn't really know him.

I was excited about the move and I wasn't disappointed; it proved to be a great move for me, both personally and professionally.

I was living in a nice part of the world, playing for a team that was a real contender, and my spare time saw me doing up my new house while, living close to Gower, I could throw myself into the outdoors kind of life I'd always fancied.

There was also a pretty good social side at the Ospreys with a lot of single guys, enjoying life and all living within ten or 15 minutes of each other, so I couldn't have asked for more.

Within six weeks or so of our World Cup exit, Wales were in action again, versus the newly crowned world champions, South Africa.

The squad was going to be in camp for a week before the game, with the first couple of days based in Tenby. Strangely, although Gareth was gone, the rest of the coaching team he'd appointed himself stayed in position for this as a one-off. Nigel took over as caretaker coach for the game.

I had a phone call off Duncan Jones, now my Ospreys teammate of course, about a week prior to the meet-up, asking did I want to share a lift? I had to tell him, "Dunc, I'm not in the squad, I haven't had the call."

Being the nice guy he is, Duncan was mortified – he said, he hadn't imagined I wouldn't be involved.

Off the back of the defeat against Fiji, to miss out now seemed a kick in the guts, but I had obviously learned my lesson from past experiences and held my tongue, knowing as I did by then that things would move on pretty quickly.

I'd moved to the Ospreys because I wanted to be competing for silverware, and, in truth, our league form in that first season was a disappointment, and we only finished a few points ahead of the Dragons.

It was in the cups we really excelled though, progressing through the group stages of both the Heineken and the EDF (Anglo Welsh) without any difficulty.

After defeating Bourgoin out in France at the end of January

93

to qualify for the last eight in Europe, I was one of 14 Ospreys who headed off to the Vale for a first Six Nations under yet another new head coach.

New Zealander Warren Gatland was in charge, someone who had enjoyed huge success with Wasps earlier in the decade, winning English leagues and Heineken Cups.

After the disappointment of the World Cup, it had to be better for Wales this time, hadn't it?

Warren actually arrived in Wales in the January, so he only had something like three weeks' prep before our opening game at Twickenham at the start of February.

Clearly that wasn't really enough time to get a full understanding of what he had at his disposal, to really work out what were the best partnerships and who would be best suited to playing the game his way, that kind of thing.

He didn't change a great deal how we did things. From the very first training session it clearly wasn't about splitting the atom, or reinventing the wheel. The difference was in the intensity and in the preparation, the level of detail involved.

His masterstroke, for want of a better word, was to basically pick the Ospreys boys en bloc. Thirteen of us were in the starting 15, with a 14th on the bench. Of the starting 15, only Mark Jones (Scarlets) on the wing and Martyn Williams (Blues) in the back row weren't from the Ospreys.

He's clearly never been afraid of controversy, with his Lions selection in 2013 a prime example of that, but this was the first time we saw it in Wales.

At the Ospreys we'd been on the a good run and confidence was high so why not go for players who knew each other's game inside out, who trusted each other, and who were, at that point in time, used to winning big matches? We were the form team in Wales, and he obviously thought that was a good way to go.

I'll tell you what, though, it was a tough old first half at Twickenham.

Going into the game, a lot had been made about us not

having won there in 20 years and we were definitely up against it. We were hanging on the ropes and went in at half-time trailing by ten at 16–6. It probably should have been more but we were thankful for the TMO for disallowing a Paul Sackey try just before half-time. That score would have been the end for us.

In the dressing room, Shaun Edwards (newly appointed defence coach) was insistent we were still in it, telling us we'd taken the best they had to give. Now it was our turn.

We dug in and Lee Byrne went over for a try midway through the second half and we thought, 'Hang on, we could do this.'

You could physically see the belief coming into the boys, and we looked a different team. At the same time, England deflated visibly. They lost a couple of key players, Lewis Moody and Phil Vickery, experienced players, and they were on the back foot.

Phillsy (Mike Phillips) then scored in the left hand corner and it was game over. We closed the game out by keeping the ball for five or six minutes at the end, really frustrating them.

Out of nothing we'd turned the game around and made our own little bit of history. Fiji was forgotten, it was all about the future now and the nature of the win, the sheer bloody-mindedness of it, set the tone for the rest of the competition.

Normally we'd stay in Richmond but on this occasion we came straight back to the Vale after the match, where we all enjoyed a few drinks, relaxing in each other's company.

I remember the forwards taking it easy, we were a little tentative as we had a new coach and didn't want to push it.

The Fabulous Five were born that night, I'd say. Gav, Hooky, Shane, Byrney and Phillsy. They pushed hard and I think by the end of the night Shane was stripped to just his trousers asking Gats outside for a wrestle! In fairness, Warren was relaxed; he wanted us to enjoy each other's company, following a great win.

If that TMO had gone against us we would have lost that game and the whole dynamics of Welsh rugby would have taken a very different path. They call it a sliding doors moment.

As it was, we had started to create a bit of momentum after the disappointment of the previous autumn.

In the build-up to Scotland the following weekend, I remember Gats making a speech where basically he told the forwards that we'd let ourselves down in the post-match celebrations and the backs had put us to shame.

You could see a few of the forwards thinking, 'OK, this is a challenge is it?' and it's fair to say that after we'd beaten the Scots there was absolute carnage!

A fair few complaints came in to Thumper off the back of it, and from then on in we had security with us when we went out, not to protect us but to stop some of our guys going too far!

I think that was when Gats realised that his comments were like a red rag to a bull and that Welsh boys did enjoy their beer and getting a bit loose.

The next match was Italy, again in Cardiff, and it was a big 47–8 win to make it three from three, and post-match was the first time we saw Gats get heavy on us.

It was warning time. Last week was too loose. If there was even a single complaint this week then those involved would be out. We had security with us from the Rhondda, big boys with reputations to match and good local knowledge. The rule was if we had a tap on the shoulder that was our night over, we had to go home. Suffice to say this calmed things down!

We then went to play Ireland out in Croke Park for the Triple Crown (awarded to any one of the home nation sides who defeat the other three). There was a fantastic atmosphere, fitting for such a great game, with over 75,000 people watching. Shane scored the only try of the game and we won a really tight contest by just four points.

So, we went into the final round unbeaten, knowing that a win over France at the Millennium Stadium would seal the

Grand Slam. After a 27-year wait, we were standing on the verge of a second in four championships.

It was to be my 50th cap so, whatever the outcome of the match, it would be the biggest day of my international career. That's 49 more than I'd ever imagined I'd get on that June afternoon in Pretoria ten years earlier, and 29 more than it looked like I'd win after my fall-out with Hansen.

I got to lead the team out on the day, accompanied by the daughters of the late, great Ray Gravell, who were mascots for the day.

It was a truly unforgettable moment for me given the several disappointments I'd endured over my time as a Welsh international, not least the previous year's World Cup and then being dropped for the South Africa game a month later.

It was an immense atmosphere at the Millennium Stadium that day. I felt that I was walking out into a cauldron of noise and passion, with the team following just behind me.

It was a tight affair for the first hour but we cut loose in the last quarter, Shane scoring a try which set a new all-time Welsh record and Martyn Williams also grabbing one in the dying minutes to spark wild celebrations.

After my cameo in 2005, being involved in every game this time around meant that I could really treasure this one. I could call myself a Grand Slam winner without thinking I was cheating everyone. That's what it meant to me.

If ever I'm interviewed about my career, or if I'm doing a Q&A at a function or dinner somewhere, and I'm asked the question, I will always pick that day, Saturday, 15 March 2008, as the pinnacle of my Test career.

It was a day where everything fell into place and if I'd died that day then I would have gone to meet my maker as a happy and contented fellow, I can tell you that for sure.

Looking back at that campaign, it's incredible to think how far we came in a short period of time under Warren. Having started with 13 Ospreys against England, he did change things around over the five games as he got to know the squad better, but we still had 11 starting in the French game with another three on the bench.

It also left everybody wondering what could have been at the World Cup.

Off the back of that wonderful experience, us Ospreys headed back west in great spirits, ready to prepare for two huge, back-to-back games against Saracens.

Fate had drawn us against the Sarries in both knock-out competitions, first up in the EDF semi-final at the Millennium Stadium, and then a couple of weeks later, in the Heineken quarter-final at their ground, Vicarage Road in Watford.

Saracens' season had been pretty much a replica of ours. They were a little disappointing in the league but, obviously, showing up well in cup competition.

Lyn hadn't used me much in the EDF, he'd rested me, so I sat out the first game, in Cardiff. I was part of a 40,000 plus crowd at the Millennium that day and it really was great to watch as we blew them away, scoring four tries to win 30–3.

A young man called Dan Biggar made his debut off the bench late on that afternoon.

Biggs' has this persona where people see him on the pitch flapping his arms about and having a go at everybody. He's very combative at times as well.

Although he's been huge for the Ospreys in the seven years since, is loved by the Liberty Stadium crowd and is the region's all-time points' scorer, it's fair to say that he's endured a love/hate relationship with Welsh rugby fans in general, and the press at times, because of his in-game persona I suppose. But off the pitch you see a completely different side of him.

He's a really caring bloke, he's a really moral bloke and is a genuinely good guy. He's just super, super competitive and I feel that's something that sometimes doesn't sit well with the Welsh psyche. People here seem to prefer plucky losers than a teenager prepared to tell and show the world how good he is.

The part he struggled with early in his career was how to keep a lid on it. If he had been brought over from somewhere like New Zealand with that attitude, people would be saying, "Well, that's the difference between us and them, that's what makes them the best in the world." But because he's one of 'us' people struggle to accept it; it makes him cocky or arrogant in some people's eyes and that's not the case.

After you defeat a team, like we beat Saracens at the Millennium, there's always the danger that you can be complacent the next time you play them. That next time was at Vicarage Road in 15 days' time and, I'm afraid to say, with hindsight, that complacency did creep in.

It was an early Sunday lunchtime kick-off so we should really have been tucked up in bed nice and early on the Saturday, but I remember the night before the match, there were a few card schools going, some of the boys were drinking coffee.

Nothing wild to be fair, but not the best preparation for such a big game at midday the next day.

The press had built us up all that week – off the back of the Ospreys' contribution to the Grand Slam and the result a fortnight earlier – there could only be one winner in the eyes of the media. It was a foregone conclusion, they said.

To this day I'd say we were the better team on the team sheet, but they scrapped for everything. They were the typical wounded animal; they were in many ways like the Dragons team I'd been part of in those first couple of seasons, punching above their weight, and on that day the Ospreys didn't add up to the sum of our parts.

Quite simply, I think there were too many in the group who went into the game without that fire in the belly that you have to have in big games.

As happens on days like that, every bounce of the ball went Saracens' way; their try came from a clearance kick that was touched in flight, playing all their boys onside, and they took full advantage.

It was a very disappointing day, particularly after the way the EDF game had gone.

I always find the back-to-back European group games difficult. When you've had a good pasting, what better motivation is there when you are going up against the same team the next week? Likewise, if you were the winners, the hardest thing for a coach is to keep a lid on things and keep people focused. That is the difference between good teams and great teams.

I played in a Newport team that lost by 70-odd points in Sale and then beat them in the return fixture. When you lose by 70 points, the winning team is clearly that much better than you, but if they are a percentage or two off their best because of complacency, and the other team raise their game just a few per cent, then anything can happen. We found that out for ourselves at Vicarage Road as Saracens won 19–10, a late try from Paul James making it look closer than it was in reality.

That game put things in perspective for everybody quite quickly, and knocked the complacency out of us. I remember that off the back of the defeat there was a lot of pressure on Lyn and he had to answer questions from the press about his future, but there was a big game on the horizon to refocus us.

We couldn't afford to feel sorry for ourselves as six days after the defeat to Saracens we had the small matter of an EDF Cup final against Leicester at Twickenham in front of 65,000 people!

Twelve months earlier the two teams had met at the same stadium in the same stage of the competition, in what turned out to be an incredible game.

At that point I knew I was signing for the Ospreys and had spent the weekend house-hunting in Swansea, and watched the game on the big screen in a café on the seafront at Llangennith on Gower.

Leicester had gone in at half-time with a big lead but the Ospreys had fought their way back. It was real Barbarians stuff, tries being scored from everywhere and, eventually, Leicester rightly won it by six points, scoring five tries to the Ospreys' four. Talk about whetting my appetite for the move!

Fast forward a year and the two teams were going head-to-head again, and this time I was involved, albeit named on the bench.

Whenever you play Leicester you know you are in for a physical confrontation. They are an aggressive, bully-boy kind of team by nature. They play with that edge, and from talking to people involved at the club over the years that's how they train also.

The prep going into this game was so much better than the previous week. The units had done their work, they knew who they were up against and what they had to do to combat their strengths. Nothing was left to chance and as a result the performance on the day was that much better than the previous week.

Right from the start we were in control.

There was a big crowd, but it wasn't like going to Leicester to play at Welford Road, where they have an intimidating crowd sitting right on top of you. This was Twickenham, a neutral venue, which took that edge away and it was a ground where most of the team had won in red shirts just two months earlier.

The boys played superbly. I got on for the last ten minutes or so, and the result was a deserved 23–6 victory, which meant I had my hands on silverware in my first season as an Osprey, and the first I had won in any form since that Welsh Cup win in 2001 with Newport.

The star of the day was Andrew Bishop. He played incredibly well in the centre, won man of match and scored a try. He has always been an unsung hero, even to this day as the most capped Osprey of all time, probably because he is so quiet and unassuming off the pitch.

He's a real tough guy who would go to war for you, but a skilful player also, which makes for quite a combination.

That night, over a beer in Richmond, I sat back and reflected on the move from the Dragons with what you'd call reserved satisfaction. Yes, we'd won the EDF, and it was taken very seriously in those days, but it was very much the third-ranking competition we were in.

We were low down in the league and, although we had got to the quarter-finals in Europe, that had proven to be a disappointing experience in the end. I suppose tasting a little bit of success had made me hungry for more.

I think with the exception of two years under Tommy Turner at the end of my time at the Dragons, I had experienced a different coach every year in my time as a professional player. Heading to the Ospreys under Lyn, who had now led the Ospreys to one cup and two league wins, I expected that to change.

However, as the season drew to a close there was news that he was moving on at the end of his contract, along with strength and conditioning coach Huw Bevan, who went on to have huge success with the England cricket team, and Kevin Hopkins, the team manager.

I had been intrigued to work with Lyn, based entirely on what I'd seen of his public persona and I was disappointed that he was moving on after just a year. Bevs as well. I'd really looked forward to working with them. I think we'd all seen some ominous signs after the Saracens defeat but it still came as something of a shock after the way we bounced back against Leicester.

The feeling I got was that he had worked with a lot of the boys for quite some time by then and maybe some of the relationships were starting to go a little bit stale, which can happen.

The Ospreys were driven by a desire for success, that's one of the things that had drawn me there, and I suppose although we had won the EDF that year it wasn't the primary focus for the people involved.

By that stage, rightly or wrongly, the bar had been set higher by the board and they wanted bigger things.

CHAPTER 8

Nobody is undroppable

THAT SUMMER WALES were heading out to South Africa for two Tests as Six Nations champions, a position far removed from the last time I'd traveled there as a Welsh tourist, ten years before.

First up though we had the unusual prospect of an end-of-season fitness camp over in Ireland. We went out there thinking it was going to be a bit of a jolly but it was a savage week. We found out for the first time exactly how hard Gats likes to push the boys physically. I don't think I'm overstating my case when I say it was a week from hell.

Off the back of that trip, off we went to South Africa thinking, 'Great we are going down there to take the series and show what the best in Europe are all about.'

They flew us into Cape Town, where we trained at sea level for the week and then we travelled to Bloemfontein, up to the Highveld for the game. Now, the sports scientists had the evidence in their hands that apparently said that a schedule like that wouldn't affect you.

Well, I'm no sports scientist but I'd beg to differ. As an asthmatic since birth, I just couldn't cope. Playing at that altitude, having only arrived there the day before and not having the time to acclimatise, I simply couldn't breathe. I wasn't alone in finding the whole experience tough.

The Boks were on fire; they played superbly well and caught us cold, with my old teammate from Rodney Parade, Percy Montgomery, scoring one of his team's four tries as they won 43–17.

It was quite a reality check as we'd been playing so well and got taught a lesson out there. We didn't give a good account of ourselves at all.

For the second Test a week later we returned to Pretoria, scene of the 1998 massacre, but this was a far closer affair. We were in with a real chance of winning it right until late on, and were actually leading inside the final 20 minutes. Ultimately though it was the same old story and we ended up conceding some late tries to lose 37–21.

Back at the Ospreys, with Lyn Jones gone, the search was on for a long-term replacement but, temporarily at least, two people already at the Ospreys took up the reins.

Sean Holley had been Lyn's assistant since day one, while Jonathan Humphreys, my former Wales colleague, was now forwards coach with the Ospreys.

Together they were tasked with holding everything together while Andrew Hore, someone else I knew from Wales camp, carried out the job of finding a more permanent replacement, his first task after joining the Ospreys from the New Zealand Rugby Union earlier that year to head up all rugby operations.

As a player and as my captain with Wales, I'd always found Humph quite hard to get on with. I've already highlighted how he was the complete opposite of Garin Jenkins, his rival for the number two shirt, someone who always had a word for everybody and would befriend you as soon as you arrived in camp for the first time.

Humph was there to do a job, not make friends, and he stuck within his Cardiff-centric circle, not really concerned what people thought of him as a person.

When I was at the Dragons, and after Humph had started at the Ospreys, you'd see him on the touchline, a pretty intense figure clutching his clipboard, and I had the same impression of him, as when he was Wales captain.

Turning up at the Ospreys a year earlier, I'd seen a different side to the bloke and had grown to really like him. He was a bloody good bloke, to be fair to him. He worked hard, was very thorough in what he did, and was always striving to be better. He was someone who expected the highest standards, of himself and those around him.

That season, 2008/09, was to prove a very frustrating year though, for all concerned at the Ospreys.

The search for Lyn's replacement seemed to run and run and I've never seen two coaches work as hard as Sean and Humph did.

They'd lost a couple of guys from the management team from the previous season and were holding the fort without any additional help, doing their own jobs and the jobs of those who'd moved on. They worked incredibly long hours, leading the senior team, working with the age-grade coaches in the evening, assisting club coaches.

The workload was quite brutal. There was an incredible amount of expectation on their shoulders from the powers that be who were pulling the strings, but it was unrealistic to expect two young coaches to cope with the workload without extra support.

Sean was Mr Osprey; he had been there since day one and was proud to be leading his own region. A real rugby thinker, he was a hard worker and a good planner but I felt he was stifled that year by what was being demanded of him while the replacement for Lyn was sought.

We started the season like a house on fire but the energy at the start of the year soon faded and it became a bit of a long haul. We just ran out of steam. I wouldn't say monotony kicked in but we'd definitely lost that spark long before the end of the season. In truth, come the start of April, the end of the season couldn't come soon enough.

The positive start we'd made ensured that our league finishing was better, up in fourth place, and we did progress in the cups again, but we couldn't match or improve on the previous year.

In the EDF, we lost a bizarre semi-final against Gloucester

in Coventry, totally and utterly dominating just about every aspect of the game yet losing 17–0; then two weeks later we went to Munster for a European Cup quarter-final, having beaten Leicester in front of a big crowd at the Liberty to book a last-eight place.

It's hard to put my finger on any particular reason – we went there as best prepared as we could be – but we weren't quite there and ended up on the wrong end of a 43–9 defeat.

Is there a feeling of an opportunity lost that year? I don't know. Losing to Munster rankles less than the previous year because of the nature of that one and the turnaround versus Saracens. That defeat was smack in the middle of two excellent performances and you can't help but think, what if?

In 2009 it was different. I know a lot of people looked at it and identified that we would have had a home semi-final if we'd beaten Munster, and suggested that meant it should have been our year.

The truth is we were well beaten by a much better Munster team on the day, with big game players like Paul O'Connell, Doug Howlett, Jerry Flannery and Alan Quinlan, and can have no complaints. All we could do was dust ourselves down and look to go again the following year.

Meanwhile, I'd remained a regular feature in Gats' squads, and we'd enjoyed a pretty good autumn with a narrow five-point defeat to South Africa and a win against Australia the highlights.

Then the 2009 Six Nations saw us go close to winning the Triple Crown and, also, retaining our title. Having lost by five points in France in Round 3, a Grand Slam was out of the question, but we went into the final game against Ireland with a real chance of finishing top again.

At the end of a seesaw contest, and just two minutes after we'd gone in front and seemingly won it, Ronan O'Gara struck a drop goal to put them two clear with just two minutes remaining.

However, we still had a chance to win the game, although the points' difference meant we'd have had to settle for the Triple Crown and second place, with Ireland clinging on to narrowly take the title despite a defeat.

Everything hinged on a long-range Stephen Jones penalty, the last kick of the game.

It was a long way out but seemed to be within Gavin Henson's range. It was very similar to his famous kick against England four years earlier that kick-started the 2005 Grand Slam, but he didn't feel confident enough to kick it.

Steve said he'd have a go, and he was a super accurate kicker, but everybody knew that was just out of his range. Ultimately it scraped under the bar. It was probably a yard out of his range whereas I would have said Gav had another ten yards on him. But, he said he didn't fancy it and we had to accept that.

That miss not only underlined Ireland's title, it secured their first Grand Slam in 61 years, my Ospreys colleague Tommy Bowe celebrating his part in a famous win having scored their first try.

Having come so close to back-to-back titles, results on that final weekend meant that we finished down in fourth place. Definitely, it was a case of the record books not showing the full story of a season.

I'd started four of the five games and, despite being 32 now, felt that I was probably enjoying the best form of my career. I certainly didn't think that the end was nigh on my days as an international and would only wear a Welsh jersey on five more occasions after that Ireland match.

As the season was coming to an end, it was announced that the Australian, Scott Johnson, who we knew from his days with the WRU, was resigning from his position as coach of the USA national team, in order to return to Wales to take over at the Ospreys, with Sean and Humph working underneath him.

Johnno is a dominant character, he's got his own ideas about how things should be done, and right away, he was like a breath of fresh air about the place.

He was clearly going to be good for Sean and Humph as he was a little bit older, and a bit more worldly wise. As someone with international experience gained at three different national set-ups, it was clear he would be able to help them continue with their own development.

Quite a few of us had worked with him before with Wales and knew what he would bring to the Ospreys, so he was a popular appointment among the group.

He's a philosophical bloke and he has quite a lot of depth to him. He knows the game inside out, technically he was way ahead of what we'd had in Wales before he arrived to assist Steve Hansen a few years earlier.

He is someone who is always thinking about the game in real depth and in his role of skills coach with the WRU he really did transform how we thought and played the game as a team.

He didn't just want people to come up with moves; we couldn't just copy for the sake of it because we'd seen other people doing it. We had to understand why we were doing things, where we'd be doing it, what exactly did we want to get from it or what we wanted to do to the opposition.

Sounds obvious, I know, but it was a lot more detail than we'd ever gone into before. He would make you think more about rugby rather than just going off the cuff.

He had the respect of everyone as soon as he walked in through the door because we knew what he'd be bringing to the organisation.

He is a quirky character, someone who would always be up for the banter, and we had plenty of nicknames for him, mainly down to his various habits.

His worst one was repeating himself. He would give you instructions, you'd think you've got it but he'd explain it again in a different way, and then again in another way.

You'd be scratching your head as you'd go from understanding it first time to looking at each other not quite knowing where he was going.

That earned him the nickname the Riddler, which became the Riddling Toad, and ended up as the Fat Riddling Toad, but I'm not going there!

When we'd be on the bus the boys in charge of the music would have the 'Crazy Frog' playing as he got on, but he never sussed that one!

In the meantime, in the summer of 2009, I finally got to play for Wales in Toronto, four years after the disappointment of missing out during the previous tour.

This one was a lot closer than the previous game, as with 15 players missing on the Lions tour to South Africa, we had a young squad that saw, among others, Jonathan 'Foxy' Davies make his debut, Dan Biggar make his first start, with Sam Warburton not used on the bench before starting against the USA in Chicago the following week.

Like the 2006 tour of Argentina, this was quite a crop of young players coming up together, which was great to see. It was a sign that, maybe, the changing of the guard was approaching.

Back in Llandarcy a month later for Johnno's first pre-season with the Ospreys, he was quickly doing things his way, bringing his own inimitable style to the day-to-day environment.

One memorable introduction was a training ground punishment that he called 'Thorpies' for when something went wrong.

I remember going on a trip up to north Wales as a full squad for some commercial activity for sponsors, where we all given new polo shirts to wear.

We were heading back south after the event, through mid Wales, and we'd arranged for a refreshment stop in a little place called Rhayader. Paul James had been pulling the strings at the back of the bus as judge, jury and executioner, and there were a few drinks going down as he had the younger squad members, and some of the older boys for that matter, like puppets on a string.

As the bus drove into Rhayader, it was like the Red Sea parting in front of us, with the road full of people. It was carnival day in the town and the place was packed. Lyndon Bateman, who organised the stop-off, maintains to this day he didn't know but I'm not sure anyone believes him.

Anyway, off we got and the entire town appeared to be out on the street, all in fancy dress. When we got back on the bus a couple of hours later, after our sausage and chips and light refreshments, I think there were probably only about four or five boys out of the entire squad who had managed to keep their polos.

Everybody else was kitted out in a fancy dress outfit that had come off the back of one of the locals – male or female, it was all the same – in return for their Ospreys polo.

Departing Rhayader, we had jockeys on the bus, cavemen, nuns, policemen, fairies, superheroes, all sorts.

As Johnno stood up at the front of the bus to say a few words about how we'd been given these polo shirts by our sponsors and it was disrespectful to give them away, he got heckled down by Tom Smith, I think it was, because it was his first away trip and he hadn't sung his song yet as Ospreys tradition dictated.

After about ten minutes of trying to make his point and being heckled by Smithy, he admitted defeat and sat down to hatch a plan.

It doesn't take much guessing to anticipate that the punishment in training was going to be 'Thorpies'.

The message went out that every player was to turn up for training on the Monday wearing their sponsor's polo. Anyone who didn't have it faced a session of 'Thorpies'.

For those of you who don't know, and I'm guessing that's most of you, 'Thorpies' were named in honour of the Australian swimmer, Ian Thorpe, and involved you running multiple lengths of the field but having to get down onto the floor every five metres and do a full breaststroke motion before getting back to your feet and continuing to the next five-metre mark.

It's quite a physical challenge, and it hit home to people that while we'd had the laugh at the weekend, there was only ever going to be one winner.

If the Ospreys were already way ahead of the rest in Wales in how they did things, then Johnno, working with Andrew Hore, were the ones who really added that layer or two of professionalism to the organisation.

The young coaching team, people like Sean and Humph, learned an awful lot from him while he was in charge, about how to make individuals and teams better.

We made a slow start to the new season; we actually lost our first two home games, which meant that we were under a little bit of pressure from the press with silly headlines about 'Crisis at the Liberty' and that kind of stuff but conversely, we were winning our away games at that time.

Things soon settled down as we got used to the new game plan and it became apparent that we were going to be in with a shout of doing something that season.

There were some titanic games, notably a 32–32 draw away to our old adversaries Leicester in the first round of the Heineken Cup, where we started incredibly well to go about 20 points up only for them to pull it back, and then, a week later, it was almost the same story against Clermont Auvergne at the Liberty. We were 22–3 up at half-time and ended up clinging on to win 25–24.

I wasn't selected in the Wales squad for the autumn internationals. I remember that I'd just bought a new house on Gower and I was moving in on the Sunday that the squad was being announced.

I found out that I'd effectively been dropped via a text message from my sister saying, "Hard lines for not getting selected, I just saw it on the BBC."

That was one of those moments where I'm just looking at

my phone thinking, 'That's just great. I'm glad they told me I wasn't needed any more. Cheers for that!'

Without me knowing, Ryan, who was still captain, spoke to the coaches to let them know he felt it was a bit rude of them not to let me know personally in view of the service I'd given them. I heard from Robin McBryde a week later.

You do get hardened to disappointments as a sportsman, you have to, you need that defensive mechanism, but that was disappointing, to find out that way after being a regular for three years or so, right up to that point. Nobody is undroppable, least of all me, but sometimes, as the advert used to say, it's good to talk.

As the season continued, at the Ospreys we were going well in the league.

The rules had changed that season with the introduction of play-offs to decide the title, the top four at the end of the year going into the semi-finals, and we were right up there in contention going into January 2010.

Meanwhile, there was a real buzz about the place as we went into the final Heineken Cup game at the end of that month, against Leicester at the Liberty.

We'd enjoyed some fantastic matches with them in recent years and the two clubs were really developing a big rivalry. With the winner of this match going through to the quarter-finals and the loser going out, it was going to be another one to remember.

There were 16,000 people at the Liberty that evening and the pressure in the build-up that week was huge. It felt more like an international build-up than a club game, such was the interest in it.

I was on the bench for this one and didn't get on until the last 20 minutes. It was a really intense game, really physical, but we just about had the edge on them.

Their scrum was a massive weapon but we'd done our homework and nullified it, allowing us to just edge the game by five points. We were going through to the last eight for the third consecutive year but they were out.

After the match there was a huge fuss, and Leicester tried to get us kicked out of the competition, because for about a minute we had an extra man on the pitch.

Lee Byrne had been off for treatment to a blood injury with Sonny Parker going on, but when Lee went back on nobody came off until Sonny himself noticed on the other side of the pitch and took it upon himself to step off the pitch.

I was on the sideline at the time, waiting to come on myself, and I remember the state of panic in our dugout.

It can be a hectic place at the best of times. There'll be instructions coming down from the stand to staff wired up with microphones and earpieces, people passing on those instructions to the players, giving feedback to the coaches from the match officials, injury updates and a whole lot more including, when things go wrong, shouting not to panic!

I think that's the worst thing to say as, when someone says, "Don't panic," what most people automatically do is panic.

It was that sort of atmosphere on the touchline, the coaches were shouting down that Byrney needed to get back onto the pitch, our team manager at the time, Dani Delamere, was trying to get him back on, the fourth official was stopping it from happening and tempers were getting frayed.

I think it was Johnno who gave the final instruction to Byrney to get on, and he hadn't needed persuading because he was itching to get back out. Because the instruction hadn't gone through Dani, however, nobody else was aware until it suddenly dawned on everybody that we actually had 16 on the pitch.

It can only be described as pandemonium on the sidelines, but the reality is that the impact it actually had on the game was absolutely minimal. Play was confined to the middle third of the pitch while Sonny was still on, and he had no real impact on what was happening out there.

It was a genuine mistake, totally innocent, but after being

knocked out Leicester sniffed an opportunity and made the most of the incident.

That was a real shame as it had been a great game; we had played tremendously well and deserved to go through, but nobody was talking about that, only what became known as 'the 16th man'.

Anyway, the club ended up with a heavy fine for not following match-day procedures. It was accepted by the governing body as a mistake that had no bearing on the outcome and we were allowed to progress through, to play Biarritz in the last eight.

The game was to be played just across the French/Spanish border, in San Sebastian, a beautiful coastal city, at the home of La Liga football club Real Sociedad, in April.

First though, came the Six Nations. In my absence from the Wales squad the previous November, a young lock called Bradley Davies from the Blues had been given an opportunity, which he had taken with both hands.

With Alun-Wyn, Charts and Deiniol Jones also in the mix, it meant that for the first time in five years I was very much on the fringes of the international scene. Although part of the squad for this Six Nations, I was restricted to just two appearances as a replacement and found myself being sent back to the Ospreys to help with the play-off push.

I could sense myself slipping out of favour. After a brief cameo out in Ireland, where we played poorly and were well beaten, I did get a good hour off the bench against Italy in Cardiff after Brad got concussed.

After the game I remember thinking that I had done well and believed that I might have just resurrected my Wales career.

The thing about Gats though, as people like Dwayne Peel, Lee Byrne and Adam Jones, to name just three, have found out, once you fall out of favour there is no sentimentality whatsoever. Once you're gone, you slip away quite quickly.

Going back to the Ospreys after the Italy game at the end of the Six Nations though, I was in a pretty good place. With Biarritz on the horizon and, potentially, a place in the first Pro12 play-offs, there was plenty to focus the mind.

If the Leicester game in Round 1 of the Heineken Cup had been titanic, then the quarter-final in San Sebastian was on an entirely different scale.

It was a swelteringly hot afternoon, in a beautiful stadium, the surface was immaculate, and it was one of the greatest games I've ever been involved in – albeit as a replacement once again.

That was from where, in the first few minutes, I had the best view in the house of something I'd never seen before and never did after, a real one-off: Shane Williams getting done for pace!

It was Ngwenya, the American winger who did it, and I couldn't believe what I'd seen. Shane had shown him the outside – he knows how to defend and was a player known as one of the fastest players in world rugby. I don't think anyone had any worries, but Ngwenya took it and left him for dead.

I don't think I'd ever seen someone so electric, and to do it against someone who was so electric himself, it was incredible stuff. He went about 80m to score and that really set the tone for the afternoon.

In the end we were losing 29–28 with time up, and we were attacking. I was at a ruck and the referee, George Clancy, signaled advantage, so Dan Biggar attempted a snap drop goal knowing that if he missed then we had a penalty to win it in front of the posts.

For whatever reason, the ref didn't give it; he blew the final whistle and called time.

It was typical of the season we were having for the game to be shrouded in controversy like that, but so, so unfair. There was no way the ref was signaling anything other than advantage. Their players were saying so themselves afterwards, they were gutted at the time because they thought they'd lost it at the end, so who knows what went through his mind when he opted to blow up rather than give it?

For any team to be successful in sport, no matter how good you are, how hard you work, or how well you play, you need the gods to be looking down on you, to give you that bit of good fortune. We certainly didn't have the rugby gods on our side in San Sebastian.

How do you bounce back from a heartbreaking defeat like that? The answer would have to be to get straight back at it, because we had a really tough schedule coming up in the league, including two away games in Ireland within the next six days, so we had no time to feel sorry for ourselves.

We flew back to Cardiff on the Saturday night, straight after the game in San Sebastian, and were meeting at the airport again on Monday morning to fly to Belfast, where we were playing Ulster on the Tuesday night. Then, we were to head south to Dublin to play Leinster on the Friday.

Again, there was controversy around this one, as the original game in Ulster had been postponed in January and the two teams had been unable to agree a rearranged date, leading to the Ospreys refusing to play on the proposed day during the Six Nations on health and safety grounds, leading to a huge fine of £100,000 and having this tough schedule imposed on us.

There were four games left to go and we were in fourth place, so well in contention for the first play-offs, but there was a lot of work to be done.

We headed to Ireland for the week minus one important individual; Johnno had been suffering with a virus that was causing him some vertigo-like symptoms and flying was making it worse.

Out in San Sebastian it had really knocked him for six and he had actually missed the entire game as he had had to go inside and lie down. He slept all the way through such a big game!

After getting back to Wales, doctors had ruled him unfit to

travel, so he was left behind as we set off for two games that would shape our entire season and decide whether it would be judged as a success or not.

We were all pretty down after the emotional highs and lows of San Sebastian when we met at Cardiff Airport on the Monday morning. As a way of trying to freshen things up and give everybody a lift, Sean and Humph christened the week an 'old-school tour'.

We were away from home for the week, taking a bigger squad and playing two games in a short period of time, and I think that sparked us a little bit, re-energised us.

Instead of wallowing in self-pity, the tour and the two games gave us a renewed focus, which was needed. At that point, the season could have slipped away from us if we'd allowed it to.

We went to Belfast for the first game and the response was brilliant. We put on a hell of a show, running in four tries to get a big bonus-point win, something teams don't do very often at Ravenhill, a traditionally very unwelcoming venue for away teams. Winning that game in hand took us up to second place. Talk about lifting the spirits!

That was where it then all got a bit messy. As players we took the title of 'old-school tour' a little bit too literally.

As the coaches went back to the hotel to set about their analysis of the game, Tommy Bowe, the Prince of Ulster, was able to locate a student night in town somewhere for us after the game and, if we're honest about it, it was absolute carnage.

The way we partied that night you'd swear we'd won the league, not just one game and had another in three days' time.

Most of the boys got thrown out of the nightclub at some stage or another, and when taxis were returning to the hotel, a lovely place out in the country called La Mon, boys were having to crawl into the place on all fours.

Without compromising the 'what goes on tour, stays on tour' mantra, it didn't end there as, for some of the group, the party went on until the sun was rising.

I remember going to bed at the point that one or two individuals were indulging in a spot of bare-chested wrestling, but the festivities continued in the team room. As great a performance as we'd put on at Ravenhill earlier that night, it was small fry compared to how we did after the game!

Ultimately, while you may never see a page in any 'Good Sportsman's' guide, advising any athlete to prepare for an upcoming game this way, I think it was an important part of that season's success, in a funny way.

When the coaches came down in the morning I think it was pretty much a scene of devastation. I remember Jonathan Humphreys walking through at about 10 a.m., after breakfast, and there were three players sitting at the bar sipping at WKDs! He did a double take and asked, "Boys, what the fuck is going on?" and the reply from a senior player, without blinking, was, "Well, old-school tour!"

Humph was horrified saying, "Oh, no, no, no, when we said old-school tour we meant we're taking a bigger squad and staying away for the week – not that we're going on the piss!"

We were called in for a meeting where, understandably, the intention was to let us know that this kind of behavior was unacceptable.

Mark Bennett, the strength and conditioning coach, is a tough, uncompromising guy who you wouldn't want to get in an argument with. He always expected the highest standards from the players and, on this occasion, made it absolutely clear how disappointed he was and that he felt we had overstepped the mark.

If you're sensible, you can look at it and acknowledge, "Well, yes, we probably did."

There wasn't really any kind of defence to offer so the boys were keeping their heads down and accepting the bollocking that was inevitable, and was pretty fair.

All except Mikey Phillips, who wasn't seeing things that clearly at this point.

When Mark was trying to make the point that there were

boundaries, Phillsy started making a speech that we were rugby players, not ballerinas. That awkward mood fell over the room, the one where everyone is cringing, trying their hardest not to giggle, as Phillsy tried hard to make his point.

Mike is an awesome guy but could be described as clean off it at times. He's a good fella who has suffered a bit through misrepresentation in the press. By his own admission, a lot of that has been his own fault, he's made some poor decisions on the occasional night out, but there's no malice in him whatsoever.

What you don't do, though, is argue with the fitness coach after a night out where we have undoubtedly pushed the boundaries, probably beyond breaking point. That was Wednesday morning and we were due to play Leinster at the RDS on the Friday. Not exactly the right time to be highlighting that we were rugby players and not ballerinas.

If Mike wasn't so good at what he does, and hadn't enjoyed such a successful pro career, then I have no doubt he'd still be at Whitland RFC where he'd be one of the real characters and nobody would bat an eyelid. It just so happens that he was in the limelight, and, in fairness, he has courted publicity at certain stages. But he is just one of the boys, and a good, solid one at that.

Suitably admonished, our 'old-school tour' headed on to Dublin the following morning and on the Friday, with the hangovers blown away, we put in another good shift. Although we lost to Leinster, we did manage to secure a losing bonus-point that kept us in second place with just two games to go.

To round off the tour, all flights in northern Europe were cancelled due to a volcano erupting in Iceland, which meant that instead of hopping on a plane for a one-hour flight to Cardiff, we had to undertake a five-hour bus journey from Dublin to get on a ferry, a three-hour crossing, and another three hours on the bus the other side.

In keeping with the theme of the week, we had another big night out in Dublin after the game, getting back to the hotel at

5 a.m. for a 6 o'clock departure on our volcano induced road-trip, which would provide a real test of stamina.

What that week did was banish the memory of San Sebastian. It galvanised the group and, whereas we could have crumbled after the defeat the week before, the run that we went on at the end of the season was born out of adversity.

We were back in Ireland a week later and beat Munster away, the first time the Ospreys had ever won in Thomond Park, before thumping the Dragons on the final weekend to secure a home play-off against Glasgow.

Momentum was with us at this moment and we won that one easily. That meant we found ourselves back in Dublin to play Leinster, who had finished first in the league table so had earned home advantage in the first ever play-off final.

There was a full house of nigh on 20,000; we'd never, ever won there, and they were unbeaten at home for a couple of years so it was fair to say that the odds were stacked against us.

We scored a couple of early tries through Tommy Bowe and Lee Byrne, a young Dan Biggar kicked his points as he always does, and we held on through a second-half Leinster onslaught to win the title.

It was my first ever league title. A lot of the squad had won one or two before, but it was a special experience for me. Collecting the medal, doing the champagne bit, it was all I'd wanted when I decided to come across from the Dragons. We'd won the EDF in 2008 but this was something else again.

That we went into the game as underdogs and were able to mug them on their patch made the success that much sweeter.

Looking back at that run, it was a fantastic few months and great to see the reaction from the team in the face of adversity. I'm not sure that it was done as per the coaching manual as I don't think it would feature in any instruction book on how to prepare your team to win the league.

But as Mefin Davies, the old Ospreys, Leicester and Wales hooker, used to say, "What is right?"

He had three young children and I think he used to tell his wife he'd be home at five, whatever time we finished, so he would always have time for a coffee at the end of the day. And, whatever the topic of conversation, he would always ask that question, "What is right?"

What's right for one person may not be right for someone else. What may be right one time may not be right another. But one thing is for certain, that spring, we found the right ingredients, not necessarily what anyone would have planned, but the right recipe at the time to deliver the end result which everybody wanted.

I hadn't given up on making one last World Cup, in 2011, by which time I would be just short of my 35th birthday. That was my focus now, but at this stage, it was beginning to look a big ask for me to stay in contention until then.

Wales had a busy summer schedule, with a home game against South Africa, followed by two Tests in New Zealand. I missed out on selection initially, and it was only a broken jaw for Sam Warburton, by now a regular in the team, that saw me get a late call for the trip to New Zealand. I travelled all the way there and back without even getting a sniff of any rugby.

Although I was playing well for the Ospreys at the start of the 2010/11 season, I didn't really hold out much hope for being included in the national squad that autumn. To my surprise I was named, but it was clear in training that I was third or fourth choice.

My only involvement was the Friday night Test against Fiji.

It was a pretty poor week in terms of prep. There were seven or eight changes from the team that had lost by four to South Africa the previous Saturday and training had been hampered by torrential rain. It all seemed a bit chucked together, not the usual meticulous preparation we'd become used to with Gats.

There was an element of 2007 in Nantes, I'd say. We were

expected to win the game so the focus wasn't on this one; it was a week down the line against the All Blacks. That was what the coaches were working on, with the senior guys who were rested for the Fiji game preparing for 'the big one' a week later.

It just didn't go well from start to finish.

I remember Biggs, who despite already being a proven match winner with the Ospreys, was still trying to find his feet at this level and had a patchy game.

He wasn't helped by a pack in front of him that wasn't giving him the platform he would have expected.

It just wasn't pretty at all and I could see my international career sliding down the drain in front of my eyes. Brad replaced me on 50 minutes and, as I sat down, I thought to myself, 'I've been out of favour and this hasn't gone well. This is it.'

They scored a late kick to draw the game at 16-all, Ryan giving away the penalty, and Gats was quite ferocious afterwards. His full-time team-talk was brutal. He basically finished Ryan's time as captain there and then in front of everyone. The changing room was a depressing place to be that night. A place where I had so many happy memories was taking a different slant.

I knew there and then that my World Cup dream was gone and that the ship was heading in a different direction.

Nobody ever told me that was it, I never got a call to tell me that they were taking a different option, but it was clear.

I was never in any doubt after that night, given the way I had become more and more marginalised.

I'm not a confrontational person away from the pitch so maybe that is my own fault. I've always preferred to do my talking on the pitch and hope that is enough so maybe I should have grabbed the bull by the horns when I saw it slipping away.

How would I look back at my 12-year international career?

Words that come to mind are: amazing, turbulent, proud and euphoric. There were ups and downs, with huge peaks and low troughs, great joy and periods of self-reflection and even depression. It was a crazy rollercoaster.

To be involved on the international scene for 12 years is something to be proud of. It's a very long time and I went from being a boy in 1998 to an old man, in terms of professional rugby standards, by the time Gats shut the door on me.

When you start off the aim is just to play for your country. Then it's, "Don't be a one-cap wonder." After that you keep setting new goals to achieve. After my self-imposed exile in 2003 I did think that was it for me but I was able to bounce back and go on and enjoy my best days with Wales.

Most importantly, I can look back and say that, while every kid dreams of playing for Wales, I did play for Wales – 64 times in fact. Not bad for someone who, as Michael Owen put it all those years before, lacked ability but tried really hard!

CHAPTER 9

Heroes and humans

THE THING ABOUT professional sport is that you dedicate everything to achieving a particular goal and once you complete it, you don't really have time to enjoy it as there is always the next match, the next tour.

You never really have time to reflect on your success.

While the Ospreys enjoyed enormous success in Johnno's first year, there was a big turnover of players after that and by the end of his reign in early 2012, I think he was finding it frustrating dealing with younger, less experienced players coming into the squad who were taking their time coming to grips with his technical systems.

To use an industry analogy, the team system by that point probably had too many working parts and it wasn't easy for someone to just step into it and know exactly what to do.

Certain individuals work better in that kind of environment than others, some understand things better, and it's about finding the right balance for the team.

Take one or two particular individuals out of the structure, or put too many in who are still learning it, and things grind to a halt, or even, at times, fall apart.

I don't think that, ultimately, that squad from my first few years at the Ospreys enjoyed the level of success that most people thought it would get, mainly because I feel the system eventually got too complex; we tried to be too clever in what we were doing. Your left arm has to know what your right arm is doing and that wasn't always the case.

After everything we'd achieved in 2009/10, there were huge

expectations that we could kick on from there the following season and not only compete in the league again, but maybe go that step further in Europe.

We'd had three consecutive quarter-finals, culminating in the heartbreak of the Biarritz game, but there really was a belief that maybe, just maybe, this could be our year.

The way we'd played in the latter stages of the 2009/10 season, with a real swagger and cutting edge, had excited people, and I include myself in that. As much as anyone, I was looking forward to the new season with a real belief that we could improve on the previous showing.

Sadly, that wasn't to be the case. In the league we were to be consistently inconsistent, if you know what I mean, while our European campaign was a frustrating one, finishing with three wins and three defeats.

As the league season progressed our form was stuttering, to say the least and, despite only winning one of our last five games, we managed to stumble over the line into the play-offs in fourth spot.

There were no heroics this time though and we were well beaten away to Munster in the semi-final, bringing a disappointing season to a suitable end, I suppose.

That summer we said goodbye to some big names, with James Hook, Lee Byrne and Mike Phillips all moving on. It felt a bit like the end of an era.

Another player leaving that summer was Jerry Collins, the All Black back-rower. An absolute giant of a man on the pitch, a renowned hard hitter, he had been with us two years, in which time he made a big impression, not only on me but on the rest of the squad and on the supporters as well.

Despite only being in his late twenties when he'd arrived in 2009, his body was in absolute bits and I think he was held together with Blu-Tack and Sellotape. You'd watch him walking about the place and think, 'How can this guy possibly go out tomorrow and play?' But he would and, invariably, he'd be outstanding.

When you talk about 'old-school' he definitely was that. He was a bit of a wanderer, and would disappear after training, or after a match, turning up in the strangest of places where he would have a whale of a time on a night out with the locals and then face the challenge of getting home. Nothing would faze him, though.

He was an example to the youngsters in the work he put in. He may have been out on the mother of all sessions the night before but he would be the first one in the next morning, you would never hear him complain, and he would put a huge shift in, giving everything, sweating out the previous night's excesses.

He was also a far more intelligent guy than people who didn't know him gave him credit for, and he would sit and chat with anyone on any topic.

Tragically, he was killed along with his wife in a car accident in France in June 2015, as I was putting this book together. Their three-month-old daughter survived but was seriously injured. It's at times like that, when you wake up and check your phone to see a text message with the horrific news, that everything gets put into perspective.

At 34 his whole life was ahead of him, and, despite all he achieved in rugby, the best part of his journey was still to come.

Going back to the summer of 2011, it seemed a bit strange at the time for so many senior players to be leaving at the same time.

With the benefit of hindsight, we now know that this was the start of a period that would see a tightening of the belt, not just for the Ospreys, but across Welsh regional rugby as a whole.

Money was tight, the regions were struggling for funding in comparison to English and French rivals, and the Ospreys were spending money they didn't have, so something had to give.

At the same time, probably not coincidentally, the people

upstairs clearly saw the challenge as one that could be good for the business. I think that, maybe, they used this as a time to try and reskin the Ospreys almost; to try and define a different culture to the 'galactico' one that had been created by the press and, I think, was starting to becoming a bit of a millstone around the neck, weighing the business down.

What was also apparent, as we went into the next season, was that Johnno's health issues had probably affected him more than he was letting on and some of his sparkle had gone. He was spending less time on the training ground and more in the office, and I think the group suffered a little bit because of it.

It wasn't a great environment behind the scenes at that time because the financial issues were just about hitting boiling point and some very difficult decisions were having to be made by the powers that be. A very public row between the regions and the WRU over funding wasn't helping matters.

Over Christmas it became clear that Johnno was leaving at the end of the season when his contract expired, the usual line about mutual consent being used at the time, and he would be joining the Scottish Union.

Quite a few of the players had also been told they were being let go as well, with some more big names not being offered contract renewals. Even some of the boys under contract were free to find a new club if they could.

In that situation it's very difficult to keep going as normal. What else would you expect when a coach has lost his authority because everybody knew he was on his way, while so many players were unsure of their futures?

We had a bit of a pasting out in Biarritz in the Heineken Cup at the end of January and it was a hellish weekend. After the game we had a bus journey from Biarritz to Bordeaux where we stayed the night and morale was at an all-time low.

I think given everything, his illness, the previous announcement about him leaving etc., Johnno's position had become untenable at that stage and agreement was reached for him to move on there and then instead of waiting until the end of the season.

It was also announced at this point that Sean was leaving with immediate effect. In his press release, he said, "I guess I've become part of the furniture. However, that has also become part of the issue," and, I suppose, he was correct. Nine years at one club in the modern world of professional sport is a long time, no matter who you are.

Nevertheless, it was a tough time, saying farewell to two coaches who had delivered success and who had the utmost respect of the boys.

A squad of rugby players, like any large group living and working together closely, can be a bit like a mothers' meeting at times, and there was an awful lot of gossip flying around. I wouldn't go as far as to say it was panic stations, but you can imagine the scenario.

The pieces of the jigsaw were seemingly falling apart in front of our eyes and it's fair to say that everybody was at a pretty low ebb at that point.

It's not an easy task for any coach to step into that kind of situation, especially someone whose total coaching experience was limited to just two or three years of age-grade and semi-pro rugby.

That was the extent of Steve Tandy's coaching CV when he took over from Johnno in February 2012.

An Ospreys 'original' from 2003, he was still only in his early thirties and had only finished playing a year or two earlier after more than 100 games for the region.

A tough, nuggety player with a huge heart, he was stepping up from Bridgend in the Premiership, to take over Wales' leading region, albeit a team that was going through an enforced transition on and off the field.

I'll take my hat off to him though; he came in with his Tonmawr attitude and really made his mark. How he achieved that, how he got everyone onside and how he pulled everyone together is a real credit to him.

As someone who had played under Johnno for the Ospreys as recently as 2009/10 and had been in and around the environment, he recognised the over-complexity of the style of play he was inheriting and immediately tried to change it.

With that player's view he had a good grasp of who he had available to him in the squad and what their limits were, not just rugby-wise but mentally and emotionally as well, and how to get them proficient at a game plan, all the way through the squad, even down to age-grade and semi-pro in the Premiership, because of his prior experience.

He immediately stripped it right back and produced something that players coming in could pick up quickly, no matter how old they were or what experience they did or didn't have.

I'll give it to Steve, I played against him for many years and then with him for a couple – and with Marty Holah at the Ospreys and Justin Tipuric coming through, he wasn't getting the game time he would have been happy with, so he transitioned quite quickly into a real quality coach.

It was sink or swim for him when he took over the team at a difficult time and he certainly swam very well. I know he likes to avoid the spotlight, that's not his cup of tea at all, he just gets on with the job behind the scenes to huge effect.

He brought back Gruff Rees from Italy to assist him and Humph.

Gruff is a real rugby thinker, someone who also knew the squad inside out having worked with the region for five or six years, until he joined Rowland Phillips at Aironi the previous summer, so there was no real transition period for him when he joined Steve; just the challenge of lifting a pretty deflated and troubled squad in the middle of a season that, having started well, was just going off the rails a little bit.

I've already said that man management is a key skill for a successful coach, not only how they manage rugby issues but the day-to-day traumas in people's personal lives as well.

A coach can almost be an agony uncle at times but some

don't get it and don't care what happens when you take your kit off, they just want you to perform on the pitch.

It doesn't always work like that; sometimes a player just needs someone to talk to, to share their concerns, or for you to be there to lean on. Most of the time, the player doesn't even realise they need that help at the time, but a good man manager identifies it, allowing him to get the best out of the player.

Quite often, especially in Wales, the public put rugby players on a pedestal, treat them as a deity, when the truth is very different. We are only human like the next man or woman, and suffer all the same issues in our private lives as anybody else.

There are so many dynamics within a team, people have personal issues that may impact on their ability to perform as they should do, but supporters don't see that, they just see what happens on the pitch and make judgment, often unfairly, based on what they see on a Saturday afternoon.

I suppose in Welsh rugby circles, the biggest example there is of this in the modern era is Gavin Henson, a man who has polarised opinions for ten years or more. He's been at the heart of some of Welsh rugby's best moments in the modern era, he's captured the hearts of the public, yet many people would say he has criminally underachieved and, arguably, let image and celebrity get in the way of his rugby career.

Gav is the ultimate enigma.

What was clear about him as he came through as a kid at Swansea was that he had an abundance of talent. He could make things look easy.

I always remember watching him in a training session with Wales at Sophia Gardens in Cardiff, where he was with Barry Davies, a really funny guy from Carmarthen who was at the Scarlets before joining the Ospreys.

Now, Gav could kick a rugby ball an enormous distance without it ever looking difficult, he was renowned for it, and, although Baz could also get real distance, he would have to get his whole 12½ stone plus into it. He'd have to put so much speed and force into it to get it to the same distance.

Gav just nonchalantly said to one of the guys, "I'll break him soon, they all break." And sure enough, they kept kicking it back and forth until, eventually, Baz sprayed three consecutive balls over the hedge into the adjoining cricket ground, while Gav was still calmly spraying the ball 60/70 metres.

"There you are, told you he'd go," he said.

When he's on top form it looks effortless. Conversely, when his confidence is low, when it wasn't quite firing, he could fall apart quite quickly. His physique was insane and his professionalism was first class. It's unbelievable how hard he worked to always be in peak condition. When he wasn't in that peak condition though, maybe he had a little niggle, then it would effect him more than it would effect others. When I say others, I mean people like me who'd never been in his condition!

It would just put a doubt in his mind and that would eat away at him.

Some people would accuse him of being arrogant, I didn't see him that way. There are plenty of incidents that have been reported, usually alcohol related, where he hasn't handled himself very well, but I saw an insecure young man with all the talent in the world but who struggled to control it mentally and that is such an important part of sport.

He was really quiet off the pitch, and a real worrier. The mental side of his game was huge, far more so than many other players. He had to look good, he had to look the part; his body had to be in the right condition, and if he fell short then his confidence would suffer. The tan, the hair, the boots, I think that was all part of his preparation so that he would feel as good as he could, to give him that confidence. The perceived self assurance that led to criticism of arrogance was, to me, a need to be reassured that he was good enough.

You'd be in the dressing room and someone would say to him, "Gav, you're looking really good today," and you could see him feeling better about himself. It's hard to control if you haven't got that bulletproof edge to you, when you have to do it week in, week out, and get through the inevitable disappointments and the ups and downs.

He was thrust into the limelight in 2005, off the back of that match-winning kick against England, and then getting into a showbiz relationship with the singer, Charlotte Church. It all happened really quickly, it catapulted him into a different stratosphere and I think at times, he was very uncomfortable in that spotlight where there was so much scrutiny of him.

I do feel for him. He is one of those who has been put on a pedestal during his career. When he's been at his absolute best, 2005, 2008, he has been amazing and outside of that people have willed him, wanted him to be that way all the time.

The kick he opted not to take against Ireland in 2009 that I talked about earlier, summed it up really. It was well within his range, but the confidence wasn't there at that time.

I'm well aware of the old adage that supporters pay their money and are entitled to an opinion. I get that totally, but I hope they can understand that sometimes they don't see everything.

The psychological aspect of a professional sport is huge, particularly in a team game like football or rugby. In something like boxing, where it is about one person, then that's easier for a coach to deal with, but rugby?

There are 15 on the pitch at any one time, there are eight on the bench, then at least that number again on the sidelines not playing for whatever reason: form, injury, anything, and each one of them has their own issues they are dealing with day-to-day, which a coach has to try and understand and deal with.

Like I said, a lot don't even try to, but in my opinion, the good ones not only try to, they get under your skin and get to know what makes you tick as an individual, to get the best out of you.

You're never going to find an entire squad that likes a coach because they are the guy who doesn't pick you, but in fairness to Steve, and to Scott Johnson for that matter, the door was always open.

When Steve came in, at the start of 2012, he had a pretty difficult job on his hands, particularly for such an inexperienced head coach in his first pro role.

On the back of the big departures the previous summer, there were more people on their way out. Some of his oldest and best mates had been told they were going, even when they didn't necessarily want to leave, people like Paul James, Shane Williams, Huw Bennett and Tommy Bowe.

Huw is one I felt particularly sorry for. Here was someone who had given everything for the cause over the last eight or nine years, was incredibly hard working, and was finally getting his rewards. He'd had a good World Cup in 2011 and his market value had risen accordingly, so he should have been in a good place.

However, he was being told, "Sorry, we can't afford you." Basically, and rightly so, the people in charge were having to make tough business decisions, and, unfortunately for him, Huw was coming out of contract at the wrong time.

We had Richard Hibbard, and a good young hooker in Scott Baldwin, so when the business was in such financial difficulty they simply couldn't justify giving Huw a new contract.

Meanwhile, he had three young children at home, his Achilles was giving him real concern and the rug had just been pulled from under him. Who wouldn't empathise with him?

Of course, it's the right decision for the business, how could they justify carrying another wage like that, but you can't underestimate how those kind of decisions were impacting on morale in the group, and that is where Steve had to come in and pick up the pieces.

While all that was going on I hit a couple of personal landmarks to be proud of. In the November, I completed 100 appearances for the Ospreys and then, at the start of March, I played my 200th game of the regional era, only the third player to do so, with 108 for the Ospreys and 92 for the Dragons.

Unfortunately, I ended up sitting out the remainder of the

season but I was able to watch on as Tandy's team kicked on to put together a stunning end-of-season run-in.

An unbeaten run to the end of the season set-up a home semi against Munster and a chance for revenge after losing out there 12 months earlier.

The performance the team put in that night was quite simply incredible. I've never seen anyone do that to a Munster team ever, not before nor since.

To give Munster credit they didn't play badly all, but we had gone into it on a real high and were on fire that night, scoring some great tries, stunning them to win 45–10.

That result meant a repeat of the 2010 final, a trip to Dublin to play Leinster.

If we'd been unfancied then, I don't know how you'd describe our chances this time.

They had just won the second of back-to-back European Cups while we, despite the winning run at the end of the season, were viewed from the outside as a club in a bit of disarray. We were certainly viewed as being weaker than the team that went out there two years previously, given all the departures.

Leinster were so sure of winning that they were already making plans for a post-match party, to parade the league trophy and the European trophy around the pitch. That says it all really.

Yes, we'd beaten Munster comfortably but they were discounting that. They were double European champions.

To go there and spoil their party, to have Shane score such a crucial try at the death on what seemed like his seventh retirement game, with Biggs converting from the touchline, was just incredible. To mug them in their own back yard for a second time, after 2010, makes it even more incredible.

It was an incredible game, one that ebbed and flowed, but we trailed by nine points inside the final 10 minutes. Dan Biggar kicked a penalty and then, with time just about up Shane went over for a try, his second of the game, that was only awarded after being referred to the TV official. Dan still had to kick an incredible conversion but, showing the balls of steel he always does, he made no mistake.

It finished 31–30 in our favour, a stunning late comeback meaning we were league champions once again, and what a way to do it! It was particularly poignant that Shane had had such a big say in how things played out, as it was his final appearance in an Ospreys shirt.

What a way to bring down the curtain down on a long career, one where he finished up as Wales' record try scorer and the Ospreys' record try scorer.

I remember him first coming through in the Nineties as a scrum half at Neath. It was when the likes of John Kirwan, and then Jonah Lomu, had come through, and set the tone for big wingers. Being considerably smaller than them, Shane would say that he had to find his own niche.

At a time when rugby was starting to churn out robots, he was something different. I'd hold him up as a shining example to any young kid coming through.

The growing obsession with size meant that if you didn't meet the supposed stats for what someone in your position should be achieving, what speed, timing splits, what weight your were lifting, all that kind of stuff, then you were unlikely to be considered.

In fairness to Shane he is probably the one player who is the exception to the rule. He had innate talent, he was outstanding at what he did, but that wouldn't have been enough on its own. He worked incredibly hard to overcome the lack of physicality and, in fairness, to overcome preconceptions about him.

It's hard to picture it with hindsight but he was someone else who, like me, fell out of favour with Steve Hansen. He actually went two years without an international cap and although, unlike me, he made the 2003 Rugby World Cup squad, he was taken as a third scrum half rather than as a winger.

I've already talked about the New Zealand game at that competition and how it had been a turning point in a few careers, and it's fair to say that Shane was one of those.

While Hansen was resting players for England, there was quite a head of steam building up in the press supporting the selection of Shane. As an entertainer – the kind of player that the Welsh rugby public love – pundits and ex-players felt he deserved his chance, which duly came against the All Blacks.

Like I said earlier, the feeling was that it was almost a case of lambs to the slaughter, but he took that chance when it came his way. He was electric that day and it relaunched his career, people stood up and took notice of this little fella from the Amman Valley.

He went on to become a true rugby legend, enjoying a long and successful career, and, incredibly, becoming the International Rugby Board World Player of the Year in 2008.

Shane has a great balance about him as a person, the way he looks at life. As hard as he worked in training, he worked as hard off the pitch as well.

He was ultra talented and conquered the world in terms of rugby really; he is one of the few Welsh players who has become a global figure, but he remains truly grounded and a great all-round bloke. He's still an Amman Valley boy, putting on charity events in his local community, and remembers where he has come from.

There's absolutely no arrogance about him but he took great delight in making players look foolish. Even in training, to try and get your hands on him was almost impossible, and what would make him laugh the most was getting the chance to do his footwork in front of a forward.

I'm sure it was Ryan Jones who at one point not only failed to lay a finger on him, but fell backwards onto his arse as Shane passed him, actually running backwards at this stage, laughing at him. He danced him dizzy.

He worked really hard to succeed at rugby and he's taking that into his post-rugby life, where I'm sure he'll enjoy as much success.

I wasn't involved in that PRO12 final, I hadn't played since my 100th appearance against Glasgow almost three months earlier, but I was fortunate enough to be in Dublin, and to share the podium with my teammates, and it really was a sweet experience.

It was a different kind of experience to 2010, one made in the face of real adversity, but I wouldn't like to choose between the two. What I can say hands down though, is that the celebrations were better in 2012.

Two years earlier we had been back on the plane within a couple of hours and, although we were home in time and early enough for the party to begin, it was pretty fragmented as people went their separate ways.

This time everybody stayed in Dublin overnight and after a few drinks back at the hotel we hit the town as a squad, players and management, and celebrated together. There was a touch of emotion about it as we said goodbye to a few people, but it was clear what the success meant to everybody.

I'd flown myself out to Dublin for the weekend, the league paying my travel expenses to allow me to do a Q&A with Leinster and Ireland legend, Shane Horgan, in hospitality before the game.

The journey home on the Monday proved to be a pretty scary experience, with bad weather and a strong headwind meaning that the aeroplane's fuel status was going down quickly as we flew across the Irish Sea at 500ft. I had visions of it all coming to a very wet ending with me ditching into the water, but, thankfully, I was able to touch down safely at Swansea Airport.

Looking back at that season, a huge amount of credit must go to Tandy. The way he had galvanised us in a short space of time, to turn it around from that away game in Biarritz to go on a run like we did and win the league, you have to take your hat off to him.

The circumstances that spring, in Welsh rugby generally, and the difficult situation inside the Ospreys that could have led to real resentment and discontent, would have tried any coach, let alone someone who had just turned 32 and was four months into his first professional post.

I don't think he's had enough credit from outside the Ospreys, from the wider rugby community, for what he achieved that season and has continued to achieve in ensuring the Ospreys continue to lead the way in Wales.

CHAPTER 10

Putting off the inevitable

IT WAS AROUND this time that the prospect of retirement, and a life post-rugby, first reared its head as I suffered some health issues that continue to affect me to this day.

The first time I'd become aware that something was up had been five years or so prior to that, in the build-up to the 2007 World Cup.

We had a warm-up game against Argentina at the Millennium Stadium in Cardiff in the August and I remember feeling absolutely knackered within about five minutes. I was really struggling and my heart rate was going through the roof but, in the game environment, you don't want to let down your colleagues and keep digging in.

I'd had a similar feeling eight or nine months earlier, I remember it clearly because it was the only time in my career I played against New Zealand. I was looking up at the clock with about 20 minutes gone thinking to myself, 'Christ, how am I going to finish the game, I'm absolutely out on my feet here?'

They were a formidable team and we were having to chase them here, there and everywhere. Because it was such an intense game, I had just put it down to being on the bottom of the fitness curve, as it were.

After the Argentina game though, I knew that it was different, I couldn't put it down to chasing All Blacks around the pitch.

As I thought about it, the only thing I could attribute it to was the Phase One drinks that we were taking before the game. Phase One is an energy drink, perfectly legal, that acts as a stimulant, specially concocted for sportsmen to take pre-match.

Putting two and two together, I thought it was pretty obvious so, without referring to anyone, there and then I just cut the Phase One out. That seemed to do the trick as I didn't have any more symptoms and I just thought that was that.

A few years down the line I found that if I was drinking too much coffee I was getting the same symptoms.

When we beat Munster out there in 2010, after the old-school road-trip, we were just killing time in the hotel on match day as we always do, trying to whittle away time. Without realising it, I probably had three or four cups of coffee throughout the day, nothing too extreme, but in the warm-up I could tell straight away there was a problem.

After just a couple of phases of the warm-up my heart was racing up to the max. I told Humph there could be an issue but agreed that I'd give it a go and see how it went.

It was an awful experience, it really was. I'd go through two or three phases of play and be absolutely shattered. I'd have to rest up while the game was going on, hang up somewhere away from the action to let my heart recover.

Nobody was able to tell because, on the face of it, I actually played quite well.

There were instances where I'd be able to do something that looked good, or I'd make a good tackle or two, but my work rate wasn't high enough and after any involvement like that I'd float around on the periphery and the game would pass me by.

The thing was, as quick as it would hit me, within a couple of minutes of rest it would settle straight down.

I came off at half-time and my heart rate was soaring, from the norm after a game of 140 or 150, right up to 220. I felt like I would after a fitness test where you are absolutely red-lining and would go to the wall. That wasn't a feeling that I was used to or should have been experiencing in a rugby match given my base level of fitness.

This happened a few times, not a lot, but enough to cause me to question my fitness.

As time passed, I realised it wasn't my fitness that was the issue and, although it didn't happen a lot over the next few years, the pattern was consistent enough so that I could make a connection to my caffeine intake.

Then, in the summer of 2012, we were out in France for pre-season, playing against Clermont Auvergne. By then I felt that everything was under control. If I drank full coffee it would only be early in the week, Monday or Tuesday, and I'd limit it to two or three in total, and then for the rest of the week it would be decaf only.

I'd been really good out in France, stuck to what had been a successful routine in terms of controlling my caffeine, but within 20 minutes of kick-off I felt the same thing playing up.

It happened again in my first game of the new season, against Ulster at the Liberty. I came off after 60 minutes and I was absolutely shattered, but within ten minutes there was nothing wrong with me.

I actually felt better than I should have at that stage of the game because my work rate was actually less than normal. Because of the need to hide from the action for periods, to recover, I was actually doing less work so it shouldn't have been like that.

Subsequently, I reported it to the medical staff, we had a consultation, the ECG was wired up and I went on the running machine.

From that they were able to identify the issue as a supraventricular tachycardia, that is, an abnormally high heart rate, caused by what they call improper electrical activity of the heart.

In very simplistic terms, it was short-circuiting, causing the heart to overspeed.

When they explained it to me, I recognised all the signs and symptoms, and, I suppose, given that episodes can last from just a couple of minutes to a couple of days, I would have to consider myself at the lower end of the scale.

It wasn't what they would describe as serious, but regardless of that, I was penciled in for an operation in Bristol to sort it out. Unfortunately, it didn't work.

They had to go in through my groin and, although they sedated me, I had to be awake for the procedure.

I was on the table for two, two and a half hours, watching them doing what they were doing to my heart on the screens, carrying out what they call an ablation. That is, again in layman's terms, burning out what you'd call the rogue strands in the heart that were causing the short circuit.

In the end, it was becoming quite uncomfortable. You need to keep quite still for them as they map out the strands they need to burn. Whereas exercise would trigger it off in games, to replicate the effect they were giving me high doses of an adrenalin to stimulate and induce the over-speed, enabling them to identify the rogue strands.

After enduring 150 minutes of lying still, with wires through the groin and into the heart, I asked them to give me something stronger to help me relax and they gave me more sedation after which I found myself drifting in and out of consciousness.

Simultaneously, they were increasing the dosage of adrenalin and every so often I'd feel the heart going but I wasn't really aware of what was going on.

From what they explained later, they were kick-starting the over-speed but it would settle down before they'd have a chance to map it fully. That meant they knew where it was approximately, but they needed it to go into the arrhythmia for longer.

The next thing I knew, I was being woken up by the defib process, with the paddles across my chest, the force of the electric current passing through my body, shooting me to sit upright.

A shock was literally what it was. One moment I'm lying

there well sedated, not too aware of what is going on around me, the next I'm bolt upright after having an electric shock put through me.

I think I swore a bit at the nurses and the doctors. In fact, I think my exact words were, "What the fuck did you just do to me?"

The adrenalin they'd been giving me had set off a full-on arrhythmia, inducing an atrial fibrillation, or an abnormal heart rhythm. I didn't know it at the time, but the defib is the standard procedure to reset the heart when that happens, to get it back functioning properly again.

It wasn't like I was dead on the table or anything like that, but it's a scary experience. I even had the burn marks on my chest, it was like waking up from a nightmare.

The arrhythmia had meant that they were unable to complete the procedure and the suggestion was that I was going to need another operation, a completely separate kind of procedure.

To undergo that, I would first have to go on blood thinners for three or four months, then I'd have the operation, and face another three months out after that to rehab.

I was 35, nearly 36, by now, and I realised that at that age, it would most probably be the end of my career, so I was feeling pretty sullen as I left hospital that evening all rubbery legged.

I'd been on medication for a little while and, following a further consultation, it was explained that if I wanted to carry on playing then I'd have to increase the dosage. While it wasn't a cure, it would contain it, and I could put off the second operation.

Experiences like that do tend to give you some focus.

It's not uncommon in rugby, or in any other sport for that matter, for someone not to have any clear definition of what they want to do when they finish playing.

I was no different, and from conversations I've had over the last few years with other players in the same position, you don't quite know what's out there.

Rugby had been my life, day in, day out, for fast approaching 20 years, but this experience had been the first time that I had to hear someone telling me that this could be it. My time could be up. I found it pretty scary, as I had no clarity about what I was going to do next.

You always have at the back of your mind that your career could end at any point, it's always hanging on the finest of strings, but when you are young, when you are healthy, it's not something you think too much about, consciously or not.

Players should invest more time in mapping out their futures while they've still got the time. I'll hold my hand up to being guilty of failing to do that. I take my hat off to someone like Jamie Roberts, who has been able to progress himself away from rugby to the point that he has now qualified as a doctor, and this while playing at such a high level.

You have to be pretty determined and have a clear focus to be able to do that while doing everything that is required of you as a rugby player; you really have to have a clear path of your future and make sure you really utilise your time wisely.

The thought that it could be time up for my career whatever option I took – because there was no guarantee that the increased dosage of medication would work – did cause me some anxious times, particularly when you factor in some of the things happening in my personal life around the same time, that I'll cover in more detail in the next chapter.

With medication I managed to see through the rest of the season, but with the budget cuts still impacting on everything, although I still had another year on my contract with the Ospreys, I was well aware of what had happened to Huw Bennett a year or two earlier. That didn't help to ease my worries.

It was around this time that I was approached about possibly getting involved with a charity called Hire a Hero. Literally it was a fleeting conversation with Gerry Hill (Hire a Hero's chief executive) as I was leaving a charity rugby game that sparked my interest in helping out such a great cause.

Servicemen face the same issues and struggles around transitioning post-career as I was suddenly facing up to for the first time at that point.

They are almost becoming institutionalised after years of doing the job and then, when they come out onto Civvy Street, they often struggle with what you'd call 'real life'.

The stats showed that approximately 70 per cent of people coming out of the armed services were still unemployed within a year of leaving.

I agreed to help, but I didn't want it to be just about PR, I wanted to do something practical.

After getting a bit more information it seemed like a natural fit for me in the circumstances and within a week I had Gerry's people on the phone to me, organising a 6,000-mile round trip up Europe's highest mountain!

Over the summer of 2013, I joined an expedition that travelled across Europe, through Ukraine and into Russia, where we climbed Mount Elbrus.

It was a great experience and I was honoured to share it with some inspirational people who shared their stories with me. It was all pretty humbling, and I found it very strange when they wanted to hear rugby stories from me, and would hang off my every word.

My achievements would pale into insignificance compared to theirs.

Since then I have increased my involvement with the charity and I'm proud to say that I'm now officially a patron of Hire a Hero, supporting serving and ex-military personnel through their transition into civilian life.

I had one year left on my contract as we entered pre-season that summer, and that was when I had the discussion with Tandy about my future and if I featured in his plans.

All credit to him, he was never anything less than totally honest with me. That said, it wasn't easy listening for me as he told me that he felt the time was right for him to go with the youngsters now; they were the future of the Ospreys, not me.

He made it clear that they wouldn't be renewing at the end of the season.

It was a first for me, really. I'd always been in a position of strength when it came to contract negotiations but, I suppose, my age and recent health issues were a factor in his thinking, which I could understand.

At that point I received a call from Lyn Jones, who had taken over at the Dragons that summer, wondering if I was up for a return home.

He explained that they had some great youngsters coming through but needed some old heads in the environment, and he thought I was right for the challenge.

I let Tandy know that I potentially had two years on the table elsewhere and he came back to me within a week or two to confirm what he'd already told me, that he wasn't in any position to offer me anything extra.

However, he did say that he would be prepared to reach a compromise on my final year with the club if the contract offer came through. This meant I would be able to secure an additional year on what I currently had at the Ospreys so, of course, I was interested.

I was upfront with the Dragons about my health issues, which meant that the move was dependent on me passing a rigorous medical.

About ten to 15 minutes into the medical, wired up to the ECG, I felt the old problem coming on and could see for myself what the monitor was saying.

They stopped the medical immediately and it was absolutely clear in their eyes what was coming next. That was the end of that. The contract was straight off the table.

I came back to the Ospreys and life just carried on for a few weeks.

It was a very strange time for me, full of uncertainty, particularly when I was being asked by the management had anything come of that two-year deal. I had to explain that I'd failed the medical and they'd pulled the offer, so the Ospreys were stuck with me.

It would have been at the end of August when I was called into the office for a conversation that, deep down, I'd known was coming, where they told me I was no longer required and they were making me a financial offer to pay me up.

I went home to think it through, to decide on my next move. I really didn't feel ready to finish playing but the Ospreys didn't want me any more. I'd failed the Dragons medical, what options did I have?

That was when I decided, "Right, if this is the case, if I'm not going to be a rugby player any more, then this is the opportunity to get the operation sorted."

I left the Ospreys in the first week of September 2013, six years, 119 appearances, two league titles and an EDF Cup after I had made the move to the Liberty Stadium. It was a move that I can honestly say was the best decision I'd ever made.

I'd settled in Swansea, a place I really love, had made plenty of great friends, and won the silverware I had craved for when I'd signed. But, and there always is a 'but' in these stories, I had this big, black cloud over me at the time, because I had no idea what the future had in store for me.

It was because of this that I insisted that the statement put out jointly with the Ospreys made no reference to my health issues. I didn't want any potential employers shutting the door on me before they'd even had a chance to talk to me.

The consultant I was seeing offered me some reassurances, in that if I did manage to find another club, he was confident that the medication would allow me to continue.

At that stage I still wasn't on the maximum dose, so he said upping the dosage was an option available to me. He did stress that if I did that and the episodes still continued, then I would have to retire and undergo the operation, but for now, if anybody wanted me, I could carry on.

The feeling of trepidation at the time was huge. I had a bit of savings to carry me through a little while if I did have the op, but I was well aware that I was looking into a big void beyond that, as I had no idea what I'd be doing.

It was a few weeks afterwards when my phone went one morning and it was Brian Smith, the coach of London Irish, wanting to know what I was up to.

They had a couple of second rows injured and needed some short-term cover.

Weighing everything up, my heart ruled my head, if that's not an inappropriate choice of phrase in the circumstances, and I agreed to have a shot at it.

It was an opportunity to experience playing in the English Premiership, while personally, it was a good fit for me as it was probably the closest club to where my ex-partner was living with my little boy in London, so accepting the move would make access that much easier. That was the deciding factor for me.

With the move ticking a few different boxes for me, at the end of September I headed up the M4 for my first experience of club rugby outside Wales, two months before my 37th birthday.

Somehow, I had delayed the inevitable again and would keep pulling my boots on for a bit longer.

The Guinness Premiership was a different competition to what I'd been used to in Wales, it was more forward oriented, power based and attritional, which was right up my street.

I made my debut off the bench against Bath, and although I only played the last 20 minutes, I felt very poorly after the game. I was sweating and was in a bit of a mess for a good hour or so afterwards and that worried me. I began to think, 'Is this it?' If it continued like this then there was absolutely no way I could carry on playing.

Thankfully, the consultant altered the dosage a little bit, taking me up to the max, and there wasn't a repeat of it.

By the end of the year I'd played eight times and was enjoying my rugby, when they came to talk to me about extending beyond the end of the season for another year.

It was a tough decision to make. I'd dropped everything to move to London at short notice.

My home was in Swansea but the real motivation had been to be close to my boy. Unfortunately, that hadn't materialised as things were going through the family court and I was actually seeing him less than I had been when I was in Wales.

I was 37 by now and at the point in my life where living in the big city wasn't necessarily appealing to me as it may have been if I was younger, either.

Then, just after Christmas, I picked up a calf injury and wasn't playing for a couple of months. As is always the way when injured, I found myself having plenty of time on my own to think about things.

I began to feel a little bit isolated, dwelling on the strained access I had to my young son, and made up my mind that as much as I had been made welcome at the club in my short time there, it wasn't for me. I wasn't going to renew.

As the end of season approached, it became clear from talking to Brian Smith, that he'd been speaking to Lyn Jones, who was still interested in taking me back to the Dragons.

The previous summer, at the time when a move to the Dragons had fallen through because of the medical, the prospect of going home, and ending my career where it had begun, had been a really appealing one.

It would bring my career full circle after 20 years. I thought that chance had gone and had put it out of mind until Brian raised it, after which Lyn gave me a call.

This time I got through the medical, everything went OK, and I was able to sign for the Dragons, which meant I was going home.

Since I'd left in 2007, it had been a pretty lean time for the Dragons.

Those lean times had started when I was still there, the

defeat to Parma being a particularly low point; they were now firmly established as the fourth Welsh region.

I don't think they had finished above a Welsh side since back in 2005.

Lyn was setting about changing that and seemed to be assembling a pretty decent squad, bringing in experienced players like Lee Byrne, Aled Brew and Boris Stankovich to support some really talented young kids like Tyler Morgan, Elliott Dee, Jack Dixon and Hallam Amos.

There was a pretty good buzz about the place and we had a good pre-season. We had a good win away to Bristol and then followed that up with a great result up in Ebbw Vale on a stinking night against a fully-loaded Northampton team, albeit it in friendly mode.

In my mind I had mapped out my final season. I wanted to have a good year, the work had gone in during pre-season to give myself a good fitness base, the pre-season games had gone well, and I desperately wanted to go out on a high, signing off in style.

The signs were there and I remember saying in the press that we had the makings of a good squad and a challenge to finish in the top six wasn't beyond us.

Lyn went even further and called it 'the best squad in the Dragons' history' or something similar.

And then we lost five of the first six games of the league season.

Looking at those games, we went in with confidence; we had chances to beat Connacht away on the opening weekend but didn't take them, then gave the Ospreys a hell of a game, and would have won it if a drop goal in the last minute had been successful. You have to take your chances though, and failing to do that meant we were in a familiar position right from the off, looking up at the Welsh teams and playing catch-up.

I suffered a shoulder injury in the Ospreys game at the start of September, after running into Joe Bearman and James King, which would haunt me for the rest of the season. I heard it pop but although I managed to stay on for the next scrum, I knew I'd done something to it.

It turned out I'd done my AC (acromioclavicular) joint. In theory it wasn't a serious injury, but it was symptomatic of how our season would play out.

Lyn was probably quite right with his pre-season comments about the quality of our squad but what we didn't have was the depth that the Irish, English or French have. We found that our momentum was checked quite early on with injuries, and it seemed that three or four positions were hit harder than the rest. We seemed at times to be down to our bare bones at centre, wing, second row and prop, with raw but talented youngsters involved in big games.

He'd invested in experience but all the summer signings, myself included, missed large chunks of the season.

As a team the Dragons weren't used to winning either, so confidence was pretty fragile and it wasn't long before the doubts began creeping in. Naïve mistakes were being made and, at times like that when the chips are down, it soon becomes a vicious circle.

Within two or three weeks of me doing my AC, we had been hit badly in the second row and, going down to the Scarlets at the start of October, there was a lot of pressure on me to play.

I knew it wasn't quite right but we pushed it, probably two weeks too early. I took about three knocks on it throughout the game, managing to last about 70 minutes before coming off.

For about two weeks afterwards I couldn't lift my arm above my head.

We were away to Edinburgh and then going into a difficult Challenge Cup campaign with games against Stade Français and Newcastle. I knew there was no way I could play.

Anytime I tried to do anything in training I was reinjuring it, and I remember falling over at one point, landing on the shoulder and giving out a massive howl. Everything stopped, but all I heard was a coach shouting, "Fuck him, he's injured anyway so don't worry about him, just play around him."

A couple of weeks later, while I was in for treatment, one of the physios told me that they intended playing me in the LV= Cup games that were coming up. I told him, "No way," pretty much to his astonishment. Until I could lift my arm above my head as a minimum it was a non-starter. I couldn't lift, couldn't catch, couldn't bind in the scrum.

Until I could do that, I quite simply couldn't play and I felt that was still a few weeks away.

If I was a fresh-faced 19 year old I might have felt obliged to try and push through it, but here's the thing, I was a few weeks short of 38, I knew my body and my limits, and I was still facing the same pressure.

Obviously, retirement had been at the back of my mind for a while now, but seeing this and, over the coming weeks and months, seeing a certain expectation as a senior pro to put myself through the mill, brought that thought front and centre.

With everything that had gone on with my heart, and then what I was experiencing with my shoulder, I began to question whether it was worth the risk to my long-term health.

Did I want to put myself in a position where I would be unable to throw a ball around in the park with my little boy because of long-term damage to my shoulder?

The decision to hang up my boots became easier and easier. On an entirely selfish level, I wanted to get to my 100 appearances for the Dragons before the end of the season; that had been one of my ambitions when I re-signed and I was on 95 by this point. Getting to 100 would round off my career, I'd be the first to play 100 for two different regions, and I'd also played more than 100 times for Newport RFC prior to that.

So, after going under the knife to clean out the shoulder, I had a feeling that I'd be calling it quits at the end of the season but the focus was entirely on getting to 100. Anything else would follow.

Unfortunately, I then developed an infection in the wound and had to go back into hospital on an IV drip, getting flushed through with strong antibiotics for a week. With my immune system weakened, it took me until Christmas to put myself in a position where I could make myself available for selection again.

It had only been a little injury and a month should have been more than enough to see me recover fully but I was out a lot longer than I should have been.

Post-Christmas I was available to play again, by which time some of the youngsters were starting to hit form and I found myself stuttering towards the end of my career rather than going out in the way I'd envisioned.

Every player wants to go out on their own terms and you always have this romantic picture in your head of how it plays out. The reality, though, is that in the majority of cases you don't have that luxury of picking what or when your farewell game will be.

In many cases, and definitely in mine, you have this fear of the unknown, about what happens afterwards, and you probably end up pushing it too long.

I did manage to get to my 100, against Connacht at Rodney Parade in the February, when I came off the bench after Rynard Landman had been red-carded early in the game.

Talk about not living up to the dream. It was a terrible, rainy, miserable day, torrential conditions, there was a small crowd there because it was 4 p.m. on a Sunday during the Six Nations and, to cap it off, we were well beaten. It wouldn't be a game to live long in most Dragons fans' memories, that's for sure.

Regardless, it was an immensely proud day for me, capped off by the fact that my boy was there watching it. We had a photo on the pitch with us both in kit, which is something I'll treasure. He was too young to know why that day was so important but it's a nice memory for me personally and when he's older I'll be able to talk to him about that day and why it mattered to me so much.

When I look back at 2003 and missing out on the Rugby World Cup, when I was minutes away from signing for Biarritz, my overriding motivation was always to play for Wales. I still had to lot prove in that arena, and I'd felt at the time that the Dragons was where I needed to be to do that.

Thankfully, in the 12 intervening years, I think I have managed to prove myself in the international arena. Whether I have or not is for others to decide perhaps, but I know I can look at my international record now and think it stands up to scrutiny.

Turning down Biarritz has also meant that I've been able to complete some unique doubles, with centuries for both Newport RFC and the Dragons, as well as being the first to play 100 times for two regions.

They are achievements I can be proud of. When I'm old(er) and grey, those stats will be in the record books, no one will be able to take that away from me.

The following game, where I made a rare start, we lost out in Italy to Zebre, a game we really should have won. A couple of tries were disallowed, we messed up over the line for a try that would have won it with a bonus point, and all in all it was a frustrating afternoon.

I could sense after that one that this was the end. The dressing room can be a pretty brutal environment and it was obvious given some of our results that the coaches were going to change things after that setback.

Old Father Time was finally catching up with me as, on a personal level, the season trailed off in the last few months.

No, it wasn't quite how I wanted to end it. I wanted to end it on a high, playing for a team that was successful, and back in pre-season I genuinely believed that was going to be the case.

Although over the course of the year we had enjoyed some landmark wins – the double over Leinster stands out, and a good run in the Challenge Cup that, where for the most part I was just a spectator – it was a disappointing year.

My final game was the Challenge Cup semi-final up in

Edinburgh. I was on the bench and I watched on as we lost heavily at Murrayfield, coming on for the last ten minutes with us trailing by 30 points or so.

I'd gone as a travelling reserve because there was a question mark over one of the youngsters. The intention was that they would push him through but I was in absolutely no doubt that I would be involved because it was clear that the poor kid was in no state to play. He couldn't walk and it would have been negligent to make him play.

I prepared all week as though I was playing and I got the nod during the warm-up, just 20 minutes before kick-off. He couldn't even break into a jog he was in so much difficulty.

There was no big fanfare, no final hoorah, but I knew in my heart that this was my last game. It was my 95th European game in total, going back almost 19 years to a 32–13 defeat in Agen back in October 1996.

After the game, over a few beers, it sunk in that this was the end. The hotel was out of town so we set up camp in the bar and drank through the night. I think at one point Toby Faletau bought a round of 60 pints, and everyone stayed up until six in the morning and got straight on the bus for the airport.

Nobody had said as much to me, but I knew I wouldn't play again. It had the feel of a farewell drink about it and, although there were three games left in the season, I knew that I wasn't going to be involved.

The focus for me now was to face up to the future. What was I going to do? I'd put it off for long enough.

CHAPTER 11

Fight for justice

MY LIFE CHANGED forever in April 2012, when my son came into my life.

I was actually up in Essex on a flying course, which had only begun that day. At the end of day one the weather was closing in and with the forecast looking bleak for the next few days we were already in discussion about canning the next few days.

That night, around 1 a.m., I got up out of bed to go to the toilet, checking the time on my phone, which was when I saw that I had received a message just before midnight saying that the baby had been born 12 hours earlier.

At this point I should probably highlight that my relationship with his mother had been a turbulent one, and had already ended by this point, so I was aware that it was going to be quite hard in terms of contact once the baby arrived.

Given the news, I didn't get much sleep that night and in the morning I flew back to Wales, to hopefully see my son.

On the way back, excited about getting to meet him for the first time, we managed an impromptu display over the house in Pontypool where my ex-partner was living with her mother, making a special tribute.

I didn't get to see him for the first time until a couple of days after he was born.

Like many fathers I suppose, I have to acknowledge that it changes you as a person. As soon as you set eyes on your first child you look at life from an entirely different perspective.

It's hard to put into words the emotions I felt when I saw him. I fell in love from the first moment I met him, and that has carried on ever since.

I was told that I could have as much contact with my son as I wanted first of all; that was on the Wednesday, but by the Friday that had all changed. Communication went downhill and it was made apparent that I wouldn't see him as much as I wanted.

There started a long process that, ultimately, would see me making headlines for all the wrong reasons once again, only this time it had nothing to do with rugby.

Just as my playing days were winding down with London Irish and that final, frustrating season with the Dragons, I found myself being drawn into a situation unlike any I'd ever experienced in my entire life as I found myself moving from the sports pages at the back of the Welsh newspapers, to the front pages of all sorts of national publications who, up until that point, I don't think even knew I existed.

My son has always been the most important person in all this, as far as I was concerned. No matter the status of my relationship with his mother, he had to come first at all times, and I was absolutely determined that I would play as full a part in his life as I possibly could.

I was part of what used to be called a broken home, I suppose, with my Mum and Dad splitting up when I was just five, so I knew and understood the implications on a child when the parents separated.

I've always been someone with plenty of hobbies, a Peter Pan almost, as the boys will tease you. With my flying, motorbikes, golf, surfing, there was always something to fill my time when I wasn't working, but, as any new father will be able to confirm, the priorities change.

Any time I could get to spend with him, even at that young age, then I would. All those other things fell by the wayside quite quickly. The priority was to see my son, so much so that it had been the driving factor behind me signing for London Irish a year or so after his birth, to be closer to him after his mother had moved to London.

As I've already mentioned, having moved to London to be

closer to my son, I was actually getting less access. It was a pretty frustrating time for me, to be honest.

I was renting a little flat in London, overlooking a Chinese restaurant and an Aldi.

On 4 January 2014, Irish were at home to Worcester at our stadium in Reading. I'd arranged that the baby would be brought to meet me at Heathrow after the game, where I would collect him and take him back home to Wales where we had a family get-together planned.

My Uncle Mike had been pretty poorly with emphysema and, after seeing for myself just how ill he was when he attended a London Irish game against Wasps in late November, I'd urged Dad to get everyone together (like my Uncle Graham used to when he had been alive).

That get-together had been organised and we had as many uncles, aunties, nieces and nephews, cousins, as we could, coming from all around the country for the party on the Sunday. I'd managed to arrange through the court that I could have the baby on the Saturday, take him to the party, and bring him back to his mother on the Sunday night.

However, on the Saturday, his mother let me know that she was unable to bring him to meet me at Heathrow so I had to travel from Reading after the game to her house in Croydon, and then double back on myself to Wales, adding three hours to my journey.

The family gathering on the Sunday was great and I then set off to head back to Croydon, in order to return him to his mother. Bad weather and travel problems inevitably meant I was late getting there. The text messages I was receiving en route indicated that there was an atmosphere awaiting me, shall we say, and there were words said when I did eventually arrive.

After dropping him off, due to the less than warm reception I received, I left as quickly as possible.

Off the back of that night there had seemingly been no issues. We'd had a further two handovers without any problems, but a couple of weeks later I had a call from the police asking if I would be willing to go along to the station at a convenient time to have a quick chat about something that had been reported to them.

I had nothing to hide so in I went; I had that chat and voluntarily made a statement. I thought that was that.

Not so.

The CPS had looked into the allegations and decided to proceed with the case, following, they said, new guidelines relating to domestic violence, and I was penciled in for a magistrates' court hearing in Croydon in the April, facing a charge of assault by beating.

Now, that charge makes it sound like a major incident, but it's important that I clarify what the allegations consisted of. In a nutshell, the prosecution case was that me moving someone's shoulder out of the way constituted assault by beating. I'll confidently suggest that this wasn't the first thing that came into your mind when you first read the charge; it wouldn't be what I'd anticipate if I'd read it, either.

I wasn't unduly concerned at that point. I knew what had happened that night after all. Nothing was going to come of it. So, you can imagine my shock when, at the hearing, the magistrates agreed to take it to a full hearing.

Until that point it hadn't been in the public domain but that was when it took off, and the bad publicity started. I can understand it – 'Big bad rugby player assaults glamour queen ex in domestic row'. Throw in an ex-pop star boyfriend and that's quite a mix. Yes, I can see why that would attract headlines. That doesn't make it any easier to go through though.

Initially, everything that was reported in the media was done from a particular angle and, to be truthful, I felt harshly done by. The implications of the charge were profound, impacting on all aspects of my life as it escalated beyond what I could ever had imagined.

Even at that point though, I still bit my tongue and kept my own counsel. Never in a million years did I see a conviction coming.

Come the July, I was astonished to sit in court and be found guilty of assault.

My story had been consistent and, right from the start, I had been very clear on what had happened that evening six months earlier.

The inconsistencies in the prosecution case underlined what I was thinking, and the reaction from the members of the press who were in court seemed to indicate that they were in agreement with me.

Although confident that I wouldn't be convicted, I was nervous about going to court and being on trial. It wasn't something I was used to. I wasn't used to standing up in front of judges. I'd been up in front of a citing commissioner once, for a dangerous tackle in a Heineken Cup match, but this was a completely different kettle of fish.

When the magistrates confirmed their verdict, the feeling I had was indescribable. I remember looking at my Dad and just sinking into my seat, thinking, 'I can't believe this has happened.' I could tell he was thinking exactly the same thing.

Leaving the court that day was the most humiliating moment of my entire life. This was on a completely different scale to anything I'd ever experienced.

There were paparazzi outside waiting to capture images of the thug who had assaulted his former partner. The indignity of having to walk through a scrum of photographers, with flashes going off, ready to fuel the inevitable media frenzy as people fed on what would now be perceived as the truth.

The 'truth' that was as far removed from reality as it is possible to imagine.

The 'truth' that now said I was a thug.

My representative had outlined to me the potential to appeal the verdict before we left court and I simply said, "We have to appeal. I have to clear my name on this."

It was quite a surreal four-hour journey home. The

newspaper reports were all up online, as is the case these days, and with the social media comment as well, a very particular narrative was already being formed, an angle that was very different to what I knew had happened.

It was a tough time, not just for me, but for my family and those close to me.

I'd received bad press in the past, of the sort that was an inevitable by-product of being a sportsman at the level I had played at for almost 20 years. Everyone has an opinion on performance, and as much as it can be difficult on occasions, you learn to live with it.

Other times, I've been the architect of my own misfortune, providing the media with the ammunition to fire with, such as my comments on the likes of Brent Cockbain and New Zealand's 'honest cheats'.

This was something entirely different, though. It was on a whole new scale, where my name and my entire reputation were being put through the mill, just as I was looking at potential retirement.

Anyone who didn't know me, or who hadn't followed my career, if they looked on the internet, the very first thing they saw about me was a conviction for assault by beating.

Not my long rugby career, any of the charity work I've done over the years, or my role with Hire a Hero, but an assault on my former partner, the mother of my child.

Not a good first impression to make by anyone's standards.

This was a real concern for me. I was still at London Irish when this was happening and, with the help of the Rugby Players' Association, they were very proactive in helping players prepare for an after-rugby career.

Through that partnership I had attended some seminars with a great guy, an online expert called Colm Hannon, who has a company called Hannon Digital.

We looked at LinkedIn and he explained how these were the CVs of today, this was how employers operated these days (forgive me if this is obvious but, as a rugby player of 20 years, this was all new to me, something I'd never needed to look at before now) and that in the digital age recruiters did everything online.

One of the first things Colm told us to do was Google ourselves and see what was out there about us. The first thing a prospective employer would do is put a name into Google, so we had to know what it would bring up.

This was just before the trial, so I was pretty confident I knew that what was out there about me at that point was generally very positive, mostly complimentary and, usually, rugby related. A quick search proved that to be correct.

Overnight, however, it became a completely different ball game. My online profile had changed entirely and I was now pigeonholed in a completely different bracket.

That was particularly upsetting. With my impending career transition, it was actually quite harrowing.

It wasn't all self-pity, though. I also had the work I'd started doing for Hire a Hero to bear in mind. I've already explained why I had gotten involved with them in the first place, but I was now left thinking, 'Do they need or even want the help of someone in my position?'

I had to go to Gerry Hill at the charity and explain my situation. He backed me fully but, nevertheless, it's pretty humiliating having to go to someone you are supposed to be helping and explain your circumstances, that it was wrong and that I was appealing against the conviction.

The whole experience had a huge emotional impact on me.

After the conviction in the July, I had to return to court for sentencing in the August, by which time I was now back at the Dragons.

I remember Lyn Jones asking me what the likely sentence was going to be. I don't think his concerns were as supportive as I might have liked them to be. It was more the case that the directors were concerned I was going to prison!

Once again lots of things were said at sentencing, and there was a fine and costs totaling £2,130, which was then deferred depending on my appeal.

Of course, the hearing meant a fresh wave of stories appearing to reinforce the negative image I now had.

The knock-on effects were huge. As an example, I was dealing with insurance renewals while I was in hospital, it was all done over the phone, and when the paperwork was sent through everything was filed away and forgotten about.

It was later in the year that I received notification from the insurance company that said they were aware I had been convicted and had not informed them, so my insurance was now void.

In my head, I didn't connect or see the link between the conviction and insurance and I apologised in writing, explaining my situation, the appeal and everything; but no, I hadn't informed them and there was no way they were changing their mind.

That led to the situation then where I had to search for new cover, and it proved to be a difficult search, as I had the indignity of telling everyone I spoke to that not only did I have a conviction for assault, I'd also had all my insurances disqualified for failing to declare the conviction.

The truly annoying thing at the initial trial was that we weren't allowed to present half the evidence we wanted to use. Fast-forward to 2015 and the appeal hearing at Croydon Crown Court, and the Judge, Mr Recorder Jonathan Davies, actually commented on this issue, asking whether the magistrates actually heard the evidence that had been presented, later, to him. The answer was obviously no, they hadn't.

For the appeal hearing, I was represented by a leading Welsh QC, John Charles Rees, a very formidable character. I was assured that he had a robust way of cross-examining and he would be able to get across the evidence that needed to be out there. That was exactly what happened.

It came at great expense. It wasn't a cheap thing to do and

there were implications, things had to be sold and sacrifices made to meet the costs.

Savings were spent, while I also had a little help from family. It wasn't just the cost of clearing my name in a court of law, there were also the escalating costs of the family court, the two things were intertwined.

It was something I had to do, though. I had to clear my name.

The appeal was listed for the January, only for an adjournment caused by the other side's continued objections to the use of certain evidence. I'd gone into court that day thinking, 'At last, today everything will come out,' only to sit there seeing the legal bill rising. The worst thing was that after going through all that, to then hear that they weren't objecting to the evidence being used after all, it was incredibly frustrating.

Eventually we were set for the day of destiny at the end of March 2015, where I was to be completely vindicated in the eyes of the law.

I wasn't even asked to give evidence. They ended the trial at the halfway stage and didn't need my side of events as there was no reasonable prospect of a conviction.

The Judge said: "In these circumstances... there is no reasonable prospect of our convicting him of this. I don't think that the evidence in this case is enough to convict the appellant."

He spoke for about five or six minutes in legal speak, laying out what was going on, and at one point I turned to my solicitor, sitting alongside me, to nudge her and ask, "Is he saying this is being thrown out? Am I not guilty?"

She took great delight in telling me with a wink, yes, it had been thrown out, at which point I just slumped back into my chair, giving a huge sigh of relief. For something that had seemed so trivial at the time, I had been through so much to get to this point.

There are people who have been through more, and who

continue to go through more, I realise that, but this was my life, my reputation, and my future, being put back together.

Walking out of court that day, I had my head held high. There wasn't the same circus that had been outside the magistrates' court on the day I'd been convicted, it was a much quieter affair.

That was surprising for me as this was when the truth was coming out but, regardless, I was innocent and there were people there to take my words and spread the fact of my innocence across the press and social media.

The journey home was an entirely different one this time as the news sank in, that my reputation had been restored. The articles generated in the press now gave a true and factual report of what had been said in court instead of a sensationalist angle.

Coming towards the final months of my career, the last few months of being known as 'Ian Gough, rugby player', I now knew that tag wasn't going to be replaced by something far more unsavoury. I had put the record straight, and now I could face the employment world with a clean record.

I'm not a big reader of the printed press myself, that's something that all sportspeople will admit to, but from what I can gather, the social media reaction and comment on online news articles was very positive, very supportive of me.

That's quite humbling.

But, then again, the majority of people who don't know me would obviously read what was reported in the original articles and take that as fact. Some of things that were said at the time of the conviction weren't nice, they were upsetting for the family, so to see it go full circle, to see the truth get out there and be completely exonerated of any wrongdoing, that was hugely satisfying.

I had needed to get this issue sorted, for the sake of my future. I'd never lost faith, I knew the truth, and I had the support of a lot of very good people, for which I am eternally thankful.

CHAPTER 12

Where next?

For almost 20 years I have been Ian Gough, rugby player.

The questions I'd been asking myself for quite some time now were, "Who am I? Where am I going? What is next for me?"

Actually, I hadn't only been asking myself those questions, I'd been having similar conversations with other players in the same position over the last couple of years, going as far back as my last year at the Ospreys.

Anybody who has been fortunate enough to play any sport professionally will tell you that it has to be quite a selfish existence if you want to be successful at what you are doing.

For almost 20 years I've always put what's right for me and the team first, before everything. You have to.

There have been relationships sacrificed in the past because my overwhelming desire was to play to the best of my ability. My goal was to get Welsh honours, and when I'd achieved that, it was my move to the Ospreys and a desire to win trophies. Whatever goal you set, if you are fortunate enough to achieve it you're still not satisfied, you set another new target.

That can be very difficult for someone else to live with.

For as long as I can remember, rugby was what I did. I woke up on a Monday morning, put my tracksuit on, and went training. We had our schedule set out for us, we were told where to go, when to go there, what to do, and even what to wear. We had our commercial duties, community work, everything was mapped out for us and we didn't have to worry about anything.

The question of 'What next?' caused me quite a bit of anxiety over the last couple of years of my career, but I wasn't alone in that.

I remember chatting with an international colleague, someone who is much loved with a very high profile, and I was hearing the same thing off him as I'd been thinking.

It was, "Right, I'm not going to be known as this rugby player any more and that scares me."

Rugby has been very good to both of us. It's given us a good life and allowed us to see and do things we would never have experienced without it. It's given us a profile too, people know who we are – and there's all the autographs and, these days, selfies.

That conversation, and others before it, was like a little self-help session because what was coming out in the chat was there were common worries, we all had the same sort of fears. I suppose there was a fear of not being known as that person any more.

I think the factor of not knowing what's next, the 'Well, what can I do?' thought, has probably meant I've kept going a season or two longer than I probably should have.

I've already highlighted how, during my year at London Irish, the Rugby Players' Association in England was very good at assisting with that transition. The WRPA (in Wales) isn't at that level, it has only been around for a few years and isn't as active.

Talking to other senior players, the anxiety about the future is clearly a common concern.

Depression becomes a problem; people have lived this life, lived the dream even, and when it's cut short it can be very hard to deal with.

It's niggled me for that last couple of years, being an older player and repeatedly being told that I'm an older player. It's probably been a slow-burn effect with me, but I'm lucky in many ways that with my career seemingly going on and on, I have had more time than most to get used to the idea.

At 26 you know your career will end some day but you hope your best days are ahead of you. At 36 you know that day is coming very soon. At 38, today could be the day.

I admitted earlier that I'm guilty of not doing enough planning ahead. My advice to any young rugby player now would be to do just that. Take time out from the everyday and think about what's ahead. Get some work experience, go and undertake the training.

Unfortunately, you can get caught up in the bubble, rugby supersedes everything and although you know that one day you'll need something else, there's always a reason to put it off – to the point where it's, 'Hang on, that one day is here.'

So, if I'm not going to be Ian Gough, rugby player, any more, what am I going to be known as?

At one point, it seemed as though the answer was Ian Gough, wife beater, for want of a better phrase. Thankfully, that is now behind me, and the threat of that name sticking with me has gone.

It sounds quite clichéd and cheesy, but I'd like to be able to put whatever profile I have earned from rugby over the years to good use. Even when the Ian Gough, rugby player, accolades start to wear off, if I'm in a position where I can do good work that helps others in the community, I'll be happy.

The anxieties I was facing are the reason I got involved with Hire a Hero. I found that there were a lot of similarities between what I was experiencing myself (and hearing from other players) and what soldiers go through.

I'm under no illusions here, I was never brave enough to put myself through the things they do. They don't get paid anywhere near as well as a professional rugby player does, yet they are putting their lives on the line every day, facing bullets and risking death, and then at the end of their military career they don't get much more than a thank you, a pat on the back and they go out into the world. That puts the anxieties I had, and have, into perspective.

That involvement has certainly helped with the transition

that I'm starting to make. Not only did it give me that perspective, it's allowed me to see first-hand for myself the work that gets done, to see what help they provide to transitioning soldiers.

That has made me more proactive in how I approach my own move from rugby to business, in terms of networking events and going out to get business experience.

That has opened a few doors for me and I'm really pleased to be in a position now where I believe I can make a real go of it on a few different community-based projects.

There have been offers to stay in rugby, playing offers even, at my age! I'll never say never, but having come so far, having dealt with the issues, ideally I want to have a real crack and immerse myself in the real world now.

As I've been putting the finishing touches to this book, I've been fortunate enough to take up a new role, as a schools' ambassador with a Welsh company called Education Staffing Solutions, who work with primary and secondary schools across England and Wales.

It's a position which ticks a lot of boxes for me, particularly allowing me to work in the community, and while it's still early days, I'm really looking forward to hopefully making a big impact with them. The company is also a big rugby supporter so I'll still get to watch a bit of rugby as well!

Looking to my future, I'd say the feeling is one of nervous anticipation now rather than the anxiousness that may have been there previously. There are a few opportunities starting to come my way and you have to realise that walking into an office on the first day of the job is no different to walking into a dressing room for the first time.

It'll be full of the same mix of characters, the old heads, the team players, the individuals, the hard workers, the slackers, the loyal ones, the ones who are just passing through and the young talent with huge hopes for the future, some of whom will create their own history, some of whom will buckle under the weight of expectation.

It's that mix which has made the last 20 years of my life such a blast.

As I sign off, I can honestly say I've got no regrets.

I've had a long and successful career that I'm proud of. Every career move I've made over the last 20 years has been for rugby reasons, I never moved for money and I think that is particularly satisfying.

I came close to signing for Biarritz, but that would have been for the wrong reasons; it would have been a negative reaction to a career setback. The fact that I stayed because of my international aspirations, and went on to play a part in two Grand Slams, suggests I made the right call on that one.

I've hit all the targets I could have hoped for. Growing up as a young boy I dreamed of playing for Wales and I did, for 12 years. I won silverware and experienced some fantastic occasions.

Importantly, I've learned quite a bit along the way, learned from my mistakes, of which there have been a few.

I've made some great friends, many of whom will be friends for life, and I've done things I couldn't have even imagined when I was 12 years old, playing rugby at Cwmbran RFC, so I have to be content with everything I've achieved.

People ask me if I would have liked a bit more money but the reality, as you soon learn in life, is whatever you earn, you always want more. That's why I never used money as the basis for a decision. I always wanted to play at the best level I could, and be around the best people, rather than being more concerned about what I earned. I think that outlook has served me well.

I'd like to think that wherever I've played, I've always given 100 per cent, and I believe that attitude is reflected in the relationships that I still have with supporters of all the teams I've played for.

You can't pull the wool over the fans' eyes, they know when someone is genuine and honest, and they appreciate that in someone. To the supporters of Newport RFC, Pontypridd,

Newport Gwent Dragons, the Ospreys and the Welsh national team, thank you, it's been a blast.

Going back over my long career while putting this book together has been a pretty emotional experience. Too often in life we look ahead instead of taking the time to reflect on what we've done in the past.

I've enjoyed this final look at my rugby career; it's allowed me to get a perspective on everything I've achieved in the game.

Now that it's complete, now that the words are on the page, I can close the book and put it on the shelf. Volume One of my life is over.

Ian Gough, rugby player, is no more. Whatever the future holds, I'll tackle it with the same commitment and endeavour I did every minute on the pitch.

Can I ask you one favour though? If you see me out and about, feel free to come and say hello. But, please, don't ask, "Didn't you used to be a rugby player?"

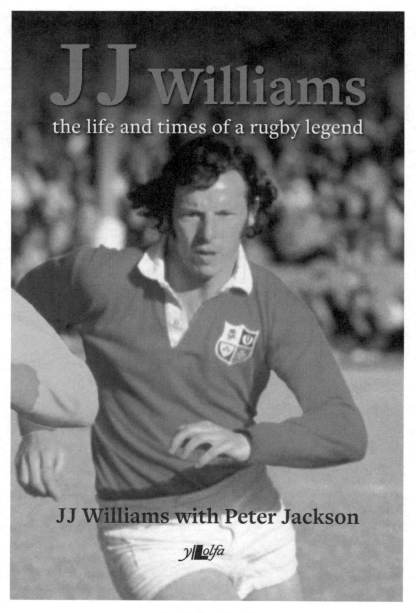

JJ Williams
the life and times of a rugby legend

JJ Williams with Peter Jackson

yl Lolfa

'A book celebrating great
Welsh victories over the English'

Wales
defeated
England...

LYNN DAVIES

y Lolfa

£7.99

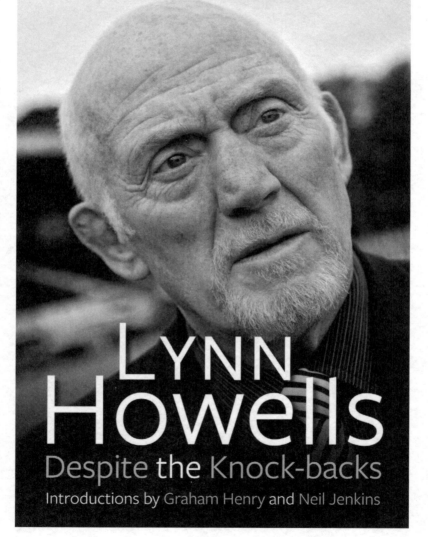

'Exposing the truth about the Regions
and the demise of rugby in the Welsh Valleys'

y Lolfa

LYNN
HOWELLS
Despite the Knock-backs

Introductions by Graham Henry and Neil Jenkins

£9.95